Quiet Autism at Work

The Late-Diagnosed Woman's Guide to Thriving
Authentically in Your Career

Masking, Unmasking, and Building Sustainable Professional Success Without Burnout

Florence Effie Wheeler

Table of Contents

Chapter 1: The Chameleon's Exhaustion 1

Chapter 2: Late to the Party, Right on Time............................ 14

Chapter 3: The Female Autism Phenotype........................... 34

Chapter 4: The Workplace Reality Check............................. 54

Chapter 5: Understanding Autistic Burnout........................... 75

Chapter 6: The Unmasking Revolution................................. 97

Chapter 7: Self-Advocacy Without Apology 118

Chapter 8: Redesigning Your Work Life............................. 141

Chapter 9: Building Your Support Ecosystem 161

Chapter 10: Thriving Brilliantly.. 181

Appendix A: Workplace Request Template 203

Appendix B: Autistic Burnout Assessment Tool.................... 205

Appendix C: Masking Inventory Checklist........................... 208

Appendix D: Energy Budget Worksheet 211

Appendix E: Sensory Profile Guide 214

Appendix F: Career Alignment Exercise 217

Appendix G: Self-Advocacy Scripts................................... 221

Appendix H: Resource Directory 223

References 227

Chapter 1: The Chameleon's Exhaustion

The professional woman sits in her corner office, surrounded by evidence of success. Degrees on the wall. Awards on the shelf. A calendar packed with important meetings. From the outside, everything appears perfect. But inside her mind runs a different calculation entirely—a constant assessment of every gesture, every word, every facial expression. She monitors herself the way a translator works between two languages, except this translation never stops. By the time she reaches home each evening, she collapses not from the work itself but from the work of appearing to be someone she is not.

This phenomenon, which researchers have termed "masking" or "camouflaging," represents one of the most exhausting aspects of being an autistic woman in professional environments. The cost extends far beyond simple fatigue. It touches everything: mental health, physical wellbeing, sense of self, and the capacity to sustain long-term employment.

The Architecture of a Double Life

Masking operates through multiple channels simultaneously. You manage your body language, forcing yourself to maintain eye contact when your natural instinct screams to look away. You script conversations in advance, memorizing appropriate responses to common workplace questions. You suppress your genuine reactions to sensory input—the fluorescent lights that feel like daggers, the colleague's perfume that makes your throat close, the background chatter that fragments your concentration into useless pieces.

Each of these adjustments requires active cognitive effort. The neurotypical person makes many social adjustments automatically,

1

through processes that occur outside conscious awareness. For the autistic woman who masks, nothing happens automatically. Every social moment demands conscious deliberation.

Consider the energy accounting. A neurotypical colleague might use 60% of her cognitive resources on actual work tasks and 40% on navigating social aspects of the job. The masking autistic woman inverts this ratio—60% of her mental energy goes toward appearing neurotypical, leaving only 40% for the work she was hired to perform. Yet she often produces work of equal or higher quality because she compensates by working longer hours, skipping breaks, and pushing herself past reasonable limits.

What Masking Looks Like in Professional Settings

Forced Eye Contact and Social Performance

The eyes reveal more than we typically acknowledge. In autism, the avoidance of eye contact often serves a functional purpose—reducing overwhelming sensory input, allowing better concentration on verbal content, managing anxiety. But professional culture demands eye contact as proof of attention and sincerity.

Sarah, a 34-year-old software engineer, describes her method: "I look at the bridge of someone's nose or their eyebrow. I've practiced this so much that most people can't tell I'm not actually making eye contact. But it takes enormous concentration. I can either listen carefully to what someone is saying or I can maintain 'eye contact,' but doing both at the same time feels nearly impossible. So I nod at what I think are appropriate intervals and hope I'm not agreeing to something ridiculous."

This splitting of attention creates problems beyond simple exhaustion. Sarah has missed crucial information in meetings because she devoted her processing power to maintaining the appearance of engagement rather than actual engagement.

Scripted Conversations and Social Algorithms

Many autistic women develop extensive mental libraries of appropriate responses. These scripts function like computer programs: If someone says X, respond with Y. If the situation matches pattern A, deploy behavior set B.

Michelle, a 42-year-old marketing director, maintains what she calls her "small talk database": "I have categories. Weather comments. Weekend plans. Comments about someone's appearance that are complimentary but not weird. I've learned that if someone shows you a photo of their child, you say 'So cute!' or 'Getting so big!' but you don't point out that the child appears to have poor motor control or ask detailed questions about their developmental milestones. I learned that one the hard way."

The problem with scripts becomes apparent when situations fall outside the programmed responses. A colleague makes an unexpected comment. A meeting takes an unusual turn. The autistic woman must then engage in real-time social processing—exactly the skill that masking was designed to hide as a difficulty. The mask slips, revealing the struggle underneath.

Sensory Suppression and Its Costs

Professional environments assault the senses. Open office plans create constant auditory chaos. Fluorescent lights flicker at frequencies that some autistic people can consciously perceive. Climate control systems produce temperature swings that feel like weather events. Colleagues wear fragrances that register as chemical attacks.

The autistic woman who masks learns to suppress her reactions. She does not flinch when someone touches her shoulder unexpectedly. She does not cover her ears when the fire alarm tests run. She does not mention that the humming from the lights makes her teeth hurt. She endures.

Jennifer, a 38-year-old accountant, spent seven years in an office with fluorescent lighting before her body forced an accounting of its own: "I started having migraines three days a week. My doctor ran every test. Brain scans. Neurological workups. Nothing. Then during the pandemic, I worked from home for six months and the migraines stopped completely. When I went back to the office, they came back within a week. I finally connected it to the lights, but by then I'd already taken so much sick leave that my job was at risk."

The Cumulative Toll

Traditional approaches to burnout focus on workload, work-life balance, and stress management. Take a vacation, they advise. Practice meditation. Set boundaries. For the masking autistic woman, these interventions miss the fundamental problem.

The exhaustion comes not primarily from the work itself but from the continuous act of masking. A vacation provides temporary relief, but the moment she returns to the environment that requires masking, the exhaustion returns. Meditation helps with stress but cannot solve the problem of existing in a body and brain that processes the world differently than the environment expects.

The Burnout Trajectory

The progression typically follows a predictable pattern:

Stage One involves high functioning with high masking. The woman appears successful. She meets deadlines. She receives positive performance reviews. Colleagues describe her as professional and capable. Inside, she struggles, but the struggle remains invisible.

Stage Two brings the first cracks. Small mistakes appear. She forgets a meeting or misses an email. Her sleep deteriorates. She experiences more frequent sensory overload but continues to suppress it. Recovery time after work increases—she needs the entire evening to decompress rather than just an hour.

Stage Three marks the crisis point. Skills begin to fail. Tasks that once seemed manageable become overwhelming. She calls in sick more frequently. Meltdowns or shutdowns occur, though she hides these from colleagues. The mask becomes harder to maintain.

Stage Four represents breakdown. The woman can no longer maintain the mask at all. She may take medical leave, quit her job, or experience a complete collapse of functioning. Recovery from this stage can take months or years.

Case Study: Anna's Invisible Wall

Anna worked as a project manager at a tech company for eight years. She received consistent promotions and excellent reviews. Her colleagues saw her as detail-oriented, reliable, and professional. No one suspected she was autistic because Anna had mastered masking to an advanced degree.

"I watched other women constantly," Anna explains. "I studied how they moved, how they laughed, when they made jokes. I memorized facial expressions and practiced them in the mirror. I created rules for myself: Smile when someone enters the room. Ask one personal question per conversation. Compliment something specific rather than giving generic praise. I had systems for everything."

The systems worked until they didn't. At age 35, Anna began experiencing what she describes as a "complete systems failure": "I would sit in meetings and suddenly realize I had no idea what facial expression I was supposed to be making. The rules stopped making sense. I couldn't remember my scripts. It felt like trying to speak a foreign language after the part of your brain that handles language stopped working."

Anna took a three-month medical leave. During that time, she received an autism diagnosis. "The psychiatrist asked me to describe a typical workday. When I explained all the monitoring and adjusting I did—the constant self-surveillance—she stopped me and said,

'That's masking. That's what autistic women do.' I started crying because finally someone understood why I was so exhausted."

Anna did not return to her previous job. The cost of masking at that level had become unsustainable. She now works as an independent consultant, controlling her environment and client interactions in ways that reduce the masking requirement.

Case Study: Patricia's Performance Paradox

Patricia earned a PhD in molecular biology and secured a position at a prestigious research institution. Her research productivity exceeded expectations. She published papers, secured grants, and mentored graduate students. On paper, she thrived.

"The research itself energized me," Patricia says. "I could focus intensely for hours without fatigue. But the departmental meetings, the committee work, the networking events—those destroyed me. I would come home from a networking dinner and sleep for twelve hours, then feel hungover for two days even though I barely drank alcohol."

Patricia's colleagues interpreted her exhaustion after social events as introversion. She allowed this misunderstanding because it seemed simpler than explaining the truth. But introversion and autism-related social exhaustion differ significantly. The introvert expends social energy. The masking autistic person expends social energy while simultaneously running intensive cognitive processes to appear neurotypical.

The paradox that confused Patricia's supervisors: she could work 60-hour weeks in the lab without difficulty but struggled to attend a two-hour faculty meeting. This pattern makes no sense through a neurotypical lens. Through an autistic lens, it makes perfect sense. Lab work aligned with her natural processing style. Faculty meetings required constant masking.

After ten years, Patricia moved to a research position with minimal social demands. Her productivity increased. Her health improved.

The change validated what she had suspected: the problem was never her work capacity but the mismatch between her neurological wiring and the social demands of her previous role.

Case Study: Keisha's Masking Inheritance

Keisha learned masking from her mother, who learned it from her grandmother. Three generations of autistic women, each teaching the next how to hide their differences, though none used the word "autism" until Keisha's diagnosis at age 40.

"My mother called it 'being polite' and 'making an effort,'" Keisha recalls. "She taught me to mirror other people's body language, to count to three before responding so I wouldn't talk too fast, to practice smiling with my eyes and not just my mouth. I thought every girl received this training. I didn't realize I was learning something neurotypical children absorb naturally."

Keisha worked as a human resources manager, a role that required constant social interaction. She developed elaborate coping mechanisms: templates for difficult conversations, checklists for performance reviews, scripted responses to common employee concerns. Her organizational skills impressed her superiors. They had no idea these systems existed because Keisha couldn't process social interactions naturally.

The breaking point came during a restructuring. The increased uncertainty and change in routine destabilized all of Keisha's systems. "When the rules changed, I couldn't adapt fast enough. I had built my entire professional identity on carefully constructed routines. Without those routines, I didn't know how to function."

Keisha's experience highlights how masking can be transmitted across generations as a survival strategy. The women in her family taught each other to hide their autistic traits as a form of protection. But protection comes with a price, and by the time Keisha reached middle age, her body and mind presented the bill.

Case Study: Rebecca's Corporate Camouflage

Rebecca climbed the corporate ladder at a Fortune 500 company, reaching a vice president position by age 39. She managed a team of 30 people and oversaw multimillion-dollar projects. By every external measure, she succeeded brilliantly.

"I studied leadership like it was a science," Rebecca explains. "I read books about executive presence. I hired a coach to help me with my communication style. I practiced my facial expressions before presentations. I recorded myself speaking and analyzed my tone and pacing. I treated professional success like a research project where I was both the researcher and the subject."

Rebecca's analytical approach to social skills served her well in many ways. She became known for her clear communication and thoughtful leadership style. But the constant analysis exhausted her. "Every interaction required conscious thought. Other executives seemed to navigate social situations effortlessly. For me, every conversation felt like solving a complex equation in real time."

The executive role required extensive travel and networking. Rebecca found herself in constant performance mode with no opportunity to unmask. "I was 'on' from breakfast meetings through evening dinners. I would get back to my hotel room and literally collapse. I couldn't even take off my clothes. I would just lie on the bed fully dressed until I fell asleep."

After three years in the VP role, Rebecca experienced what her doctor initially diagnosed as severe depression. Medication didn't help. Therapy focused on work-life balance made things worse by adding guilt about her inability to "just relax." Finally, an astute therapist recognized the signs of autistic burnout and suggested an assessment.

The autism diagnosis reframed everything. Rebecca realized she hadn't failed at corporate success—she had succeeded at an unsustainable cost. She now works as a consultant, choosing projects that align with her interests and controlling her exposure to masking-intensive situations.

Case Study: Diana's Academic Excellence

Diana earned tenure as an English professor at a small liberal arts college. Her scholarship received national recognition. Students praised her teaching. Colleagues respected her contributions to the department. Yet Diana describes her academic career as "20 years of exhausting performance art."

"Academic culture values a specific type of intellectual performance," Diana notes. "The witty comment in faculty meetings. The insightful question at conferences. The charming conversation at department parties. I could produce good scholarship—that part came naturally. But the social performance of being an academic nearly destroyed me."

Diana developed elaborate systems to manage academic social life. She prepared comments before faculty meetings. She practiced small talk before conferences. She limited her time at department events by arriving late and leaving early, citing childcare obligations she didn't actually have. "I lied constantly about why I couldn't attend social events. It seemed easier than explaining that I found them physically painful."

The tenure process intensified the masking demands. Diana needed to appear collegial, collaborative, and engaged with department life. She forced herself to attend every event, serve on every committee, and accept every social invitation for two years. "I got tenure, but I also got a breakdown. The week after my tenure letter arrived, I stopped being able to speak. Selective mutism, they called it. I couldn't produce words for three weeks."

Diana's experience demonstrates how masking can succeed by external measures while simultaneously destroying the person doing the masking. She achieved her professional goals but lost her health in the process.

Recognizing Your Own Masking Behaviors

Most autistic women who mask have done so for so long that it feels natural. They may not recognize masking as masking—just as the effort of living. These questions can help identify masking patterns:

Physical and Sensory Masking

Do you force yourself to maintain eye contact even when it feels uncomfortable? Do you suppress stimming behaviors like hand movements or rocking? Do you hide your reactions to sensory input like bright lights or loud noises? Do you push through physical discomfort rather than addressing it?

Social and Communication Masking

Do you rehearse conversations in advance? Do you have scripted responses for common social situations? Do you mirror other people's body language and expressions? Do you wait for others to speak first so you can match their communication style?

Cognitive and Emotional Masking

Do you analyze social interactions constantly, trying to determine the "right" response? Do you feel like you're translating between two languages during conversations? Do you suppress your genuine emotional reactions because they don't match what others expect? Do you pretend to understand social nuances that actually confuse you?

Professional Masking

Do you create extensive systems and checklists to manage workplace social expectations? Do you avoid advocating for accommodations you need? Do you work significantly longer hours than colleagues to compensate for the energy spent masking? Do you feel relief when working alone or from home?

If you answered yes to several of these questions, you likely engage in masking behaviors. This doesn't mean you should immediately stop all masking—masking serves protective functions in many situations. But recognizing masking as masking, rather than as just normal professional behavior, represents the first step toward making conscious choices about when and how much to mask.

The Relief of Recognition

When autistic women finally learn about masking and recognize their own behaviors in the description, many describe a sense of relief so profound it brings tears. For decades, they blamed themselves for finding basic social interactions exhausting. They thought everyone else possessed some secret knowledge they had missed. They assumed their exhaustion indicated weakness or incompetence.

Learning about masking provides a framework that explains the exhaustion. The problem wasn't personal failure. The problem was attempting to function in a neurotype that didn't match their own while receiving no acknowledgment of the extra effort required.

This recognition alone doesn't solve the problem. Masking behaviors don't disappear just because you understand them. But understanding creates the possibility of change. You can begin to make conscious choices about when masking serves your interests and when it extracts too high a price. You can start seeking environments that reduce the need for masking. You can give yourself credit for the enormous effort you've been expending all along.

The chameleon's exhaustion is real. It's not your imagination or your weakness. It's the natural consequence of asking your brain to operate in ways that contradict its fundamental wiring, day after day, year after year. Understanding this cost doesn't erase it, but it does validate your experience and open the door to different choices.

A Path Forward

Recognizing masking represents the beginning of a longer process. The subsequent chapters will address how to obtain an accurate diagnosis, understand your specific autistic profile, and develop strategies for thriving professionally without destroying yourself in the process. But this first recognition—the acknowledgment that your exhaustion has a legitimate cause—matters tremendously.

You're not failing at being a professional woman. You're succeeding at an extraordinarily difficult task: functioning in a professional world designed for a different neurotype than your own. That success has come at great cost, but it has also demonstrated your remarkable adaptability and resilience. The question now becomes: how can you redirect that adaptability toward creating conditions where you can thrive rather than merely survive?

Key Takeaways

The Nature of Masking

- Masking requires active cognitive effort across multiple channels simultaneously—physical, social, sensory, and emotional

- The energy spent on masking reduces the energy available for actual work tasks

- Masking behaviors often feel automatic because they've been practiced for decades

Recognizable Patterns

- Forced eye contact, scripted conversations, and sensory suppression represent common masking behaviors

- Professional environments often demand intensive masking while providing no recognition of this extra effort

- High achievement often coexists with extreme exhaustion in masking autistic women

The Cost of Camouflage

- Traditional burnout interventions fail because they don't address the root cause—the act of masking itself

- Autistic burnout progresses through predictable stages from high functioning to breakdown

- Recovery requires more than rest; it requires reducing masking demands

Moving Forward

- Recognition of masking behaviors validates the exhaustion autistic women experience

- Understanding masking doesn't eliminate it but allows for conscious choices about when and how much to mask

- Professional success achieved through unsustainable masking requires reevaluation and adjustment

Chapter 2: Late to the Party, Right on Time

The diagnosis arrives decades after childhood. Some women receive it at 30, others at 40, still others at 50 or beyond. They sit in clinicians' offices or read assessment reports and think: How did everyone miss this? The answer reveals more about diagnostic systems than about the women themselves.

Autism research and diagnostic criteria developed primarily through observation of boys and men. The characteristics that define autism in clinical literature—the ones that determine who receives diagnosis and support—reflect male presentations of the condition. When autism manifests differently, as it often does in females, the diagnostic system fails to recognize it.

This failure carries consequences. Women spend decades thinking something is wrong with them without understanding what or why. They receive multiple incorrect diagnoses. They blame themselves for difficulties that stem from neurological differences. They mask their differences while slowly eroding their mental and physical health. Then, finally, they receive an explanation that makes sense of their entire lives.

Why Autism in Women Goes Undetected

The Male Template Problem

Hans Asperger and Leo Kanner, the physicians who first described autism, based their observations primarily on boys. Their descriptions shaped diagnostic criteria for decades. The DSM and ICD diagnostic manuals still reflect these early male-centric observations, though recent revisions have attempted to address this bias.

The stereotypical autistic child avoids eye contact, displays obvious repetitive behaviors, shows intense but narrow interests in topics like trains or dinosaurs, and struggles visibly with social interaction. Many autistic girls and women don't match this template. They make eye contact—forced and uncomfortable, but present. They hide their repetitive behaviors. Their intense interests focus on more socially acceptable topics like animals or books. They study social interaction like a foreign language and develop competence through conscious effort.

Clinical tools designed to identify autism screen for the male presentation. When clinicians use these tools with girls and women, they miss cases that don't fit the expected pattern. The tools weren't designed for female presentations, so they fail to detect them.

Social Camouflaging Skills

Research shows that autistic females engage in more intensive social camouflaging than autistic males. This difference appears early. Autistic girls observe their peers and mimic social behaviors more extensively than autistic boys. They work harder to blend in, and they often succeed—at tremendous personal cost.

The success of this camouflaging creates a paradox. The better a woman becomes at appearing neurotypical, the less likely she is to receive an accurate diagnosis. Her struggles remain invisible. Teachers and parents see a shy or quirky girl who tries hard. They don't see autism because the girl has learned to hide the very behaviors that would trigger recognition.

Lauren, diagnosed at age 37, describes her childhood: "I was labeled 'too sensitive.' Teachers said I needed to develop a thicker skin. My mother thought I was deliberately difficult. No one considered autism because I made friends—sort of—and I did well academically. No one saw how exhausting it all was, how I spent every evening hiding in my room recovering from the effort of appearing normal all day."

Gender Expectations and Socialization

Culture teaches girls different social expectations than boys. Girls receive intensive instruction in emotional labor, social monitoring, and relationship maintenance. These teachings can mask autistic traits or make them seem like extreme femininity rather than neurological difference.

The autistic girl who studies facial expressions and practices appropriate emotional responses looks like a girl trying hard to be polite. The autistic boy who doesn't study these things looks autistic. The girl's effort renders her autism invisible while simultaneously exhausting her.

Clinicians often fail to account for this differential socialization. They expect autistic people to lack social motivation. But many autistic women desperately want connection—they just struggle with the execution. They want friends but don't know how to make them. They want to fit in but the rules keep changing. This desire for connection, combined with camouflaging skills, leads clinicians to conclude they can't be autistic.

The Outdated Diagnostic Criteria Problem

What the Criteria Miss

Current diagnostic criteria require deficits in social communication and interaction plus restricted, repetitive patterns of behavior or interests. The word "deficits" creates immediate problems. Many autistic women don't display obvious deficits—they display differences that they've learned to mask.

The social communication criterion looks for specific behaviors: reduced eye contact, limited facial expression, difficulty with conversation flow. An autistic woman who has spent 30 years practicing eye contact and memorizing facial expressions may pass these markers even though the effort exhausts her. The criterion doesn't account for the cost of appearing typical.

The restricted interests criterion expects narrow fixations on unusual topics. But what happens when an autistic woman's intense interest focuses on psychology, literature, or social justice—topics that appear typical for educated women? Her intensity might manifest as extensive reading, detailed knowledge, and passionate advocacy. These don't trigger concern the way an intense interest in vacuum cleaners would.

The repetitive behaviors criterion looks for obvious stimming, rigid routines, and resistance to change. An autistic woman who has learned to suppress hand-flapping, who disguises her routines as healthy habits, and who forces herself through changes while experiencing internal distress may not meet this criterion observably, even though she experiences the same need for predictability and self-regulation.

The Intelligence Factor

Higher cognitive ability often masks autism in women. An intelligent autistic girl can analyze social situations cognitively, creating rules and scripts that compensate for intuitive deficits. She might not understand why people behave certain ways, but she can memorize that they do and respond accordingly.

This cognitive compensation works until it doesn't. The systems break down under stress, during transitions, or when situations deviate from established patterns. But by the time breakdown occurs, the woman is often well into adulthood, and the connection between her struggles and autism remains obscured by her history of apparent competence.

Common Misdiagnoses

Anxiety and Depression

The most frequent misdiagnoses for autistic women involve anxiety and depression. These conditions often do coexist with autism, but clinicians frequently diagnose them as primary conditions and miss the underlying autism.

The autistic woman experiences significant anxiety—social situations cause distress, sensory overload triggers panic, unexpected changes create overwhelming stress. A clinician treating this as generalized anxiety disorder might prescribe medication and cognitive-behavioral therapy. These interventions may help somewhat, but they don't address the root cause. The anxiety persists because it stems from trying to function in an environment that doesn't match her neurological needs.

Depression commonly develops in autistic women by their 20s or 30s. The constant effort of masking, the repeated experience of social failure despite enormous effort, the sense of being fundamentally different without understanding why—these create conditions where depression flourishes. But treating the depression without recognizing the autism leaves the underlying problem unaddressed.

Maria, diagnosed with autism at 41 after 20 years of depression treatment, explains: "Every therapist I saw focused on negative thinking patterns or childhood trauma. No one asked why I found basic social interactions so exhausting or why I needed such rigid routines. When I finally saw a therapist who recognized autism, everything changed. The depression wasn't wrong thinking—it was a rational response to trying to exist in a world not designed for my brain."

Borderline Personality Disorder

Borderline personality disorder (BPD) appears frequently as a misdiagnosis for autistic women. The presentation can appear similar: emotional dysregulation, relationship difficulties, intense reactions to perceived rejection, black-and-white thinking. But the underlying causes differ fundamentally.

The autistic woman might experience emotional dysregulation because she processes emotions intensely and lacks neurotypical tools for modulation. Her relationship difficulties stem from genuine confusion about social expectations, not manipulation or fear of abandonment. Her intense reactions to perceived rejection may reflect authentic distress about social confusion or sensory overload during conflict. Her black-and-white thinking might represent a cognitive style rather than a defense mechanism.

Treatment for BPD focuses on emotional regulation skills and examining thought patterns. These interventions may help autistic women to some extent, but they miss the central issue. The woman isn't failing at emotional regulation as a personality disorder—she's attempting to regulate emotions in contexts that overwhelm her sensory and social processing capabilities.

Attention Deficit Hyperactivity Disorder (ADHD)

ADHD and autism overlap significantly in women. Many autistic women also have ADHD. But some receive ADHD diagnoses that miss the concurrent autism. The executive function challenges, attention differences, and impulsivity can mask the social communication and sensory processing aspects of autism.

The clinician sees a woman who struggles with organization, gets distracted easily, and acts impulsively. ADHD medication might help with some symptoms. But if the underlying autism remains unrecognized, the woman continues struggling with sensory issues, social confusion, and the exhaustion of masking without understanding why ADHD treatment alone doesn't fully resolve her difficulties.

The Diagnosis Journey

Self-Discovery Through Online Communities

Many women first recognize their autism through social media, online communities, or reading accounts by autistic women. They encounter descriptions that match their experiences with startling precision. They think: Wait, I do that. I've always felt that way. This is autism?

The online autism community, particularly networks of autistic women, has created space for sharing experiences that don't match clinical stereotypes. These communities describe masking, sensory sensitivity, social exhaustion, and special interests in ways that resonate with late-diagnosed women. They validate experiences that clinicians have dismissed for years.

Chloe, diagnosed at 33, discovered autism through social media: "A friend shared an article about autism in women. I read it and cried for an hour. Every paragraph described my life. The exhaustion from social interaction. The need for routine. The sensory issues I'd thought were just weird preferences. I had always thought I was broken. Suddenly I had an explanation."

This self-recognition often precedes formal diagnosis by months or years. Women research extensively before pursuing assessment. They want to be certain, partly because seeking diagnosis requires significant effort and partly because they fear dismissal from clinicians who don't understand female presentations of autism.

The Formal Assessment Process

Pursuing formal diagnosis as an adult presents multiple challenges. Many clinicians lack training in adult autism assessment, particularly in women. Wait lists for qualified assessors can extend for months or years. Assessment costs thousands of dollars in many regions, and insurance may not cover adult autism evaluation.

The assessment itself requires providing developmental history—information about early childhood that many women struggle to access. Their parents may not remember details or may have normalized behaviors that were actually autistic traits. School records might exist but require effort to obtain. The assessor needs evidence of autism present in childhood, even if it wasn't recognized at the time.

Standard assessment tools, as discussed earlier, often miss female presentations. A skilled assessor will look beyond the tools, asking about masking behaviors, sensory experiences, and social exhaustion. They'll inquire about special interests that might appear typical in focus but atypical in intensity. They'll explore how the woman compensates for social challenges rather than just assessing whether challenges exist.

Some women pursue self-diagnosis rather than formal assessment. The autism community increasingly validates self-diagnosis, particularly given the barriers to accessing formal assessment and the frequent misdiagnosis by clinicians unfamiliar with autism in women. Self-diagnosis provides the framework for understanding one's experiences and can guide toward appropriate supports, even without official documentation.

Case Study: Elena's Decades of Misunderstanding

Elena received her autism diagnosis at age 45, after accumulating an impressive collection of incorrect diagnoses: generalized anxiety disorder, social anxiety disorder, major depressive disorder, obsessive-compulsive disorder, and finally borderline personality disorder.

"Each diagnosis seemed partially right but mostly wrong," Elena recalls. "Yes, I experienced anxiety. Yes, I got depressed. But the treatments never quite worked because no one understood the underlying cause. Therapy taught me to challenge negative thoughts, but my thoughts weren't the problem. My brain processed the world differently than the neurotypical people around me, and trying to function in their world exhausted me."

Elena worked as a librarian, a job she chose specifically because it aligned with her interests and provided predictable structure. She excelled at cataloging, research assistance, and information organization. The job difficulties arose from unpredictable patron interactions and social expectations from colleagues.

"I could help someone find information all day without fatigue. But making small talk in the break room destroyed me. Staff meetings gave me panic attacks. I thought I was just bad at being a person."

The breakthrough came through her teenage daughter's autism diagnosis. During her daughter's assessment, Elena recognized herself

21

in every characteristic described. She pursued her own evaluation, finally receiving the explanation that made sense of 45 years of struggling.

"The diagnosis felt like permission to stop pretending. I could acknowledge that social situations exhausted me, that I needed routines, that certain textures made me physically uncomfortable. I wasn't defective—I was autistic. That difference mattered enormously."

Case Study: Simone's Corporate Success and Private Struggle

Simone built a successful career in finance, reaching senior management by age 38. Colleagues saw her as intelligent, hardworking, and professional. None suspected the effort required for her to maintain this image.

"I studied professional behavior like it was a second language. I observed how successful women dressed, spoke, and carried themselves. I created rules: Smile when greeting people. Ask one personal question per conversation. Mirror the other person's energy level. I had algorithms for everything."

Despite her success, Simone experienced periods of what doctors labeled depression. She would function highly for months, then crash completely. These crashes followed predictable patterns—after major projects with intensive social demands or following conferences requiring extensive networking.

"I thought I just needed to manage stress better. Take more vacations. Practice self-care. But nothing helped because I was treating symptoms rather than the underlying cause."

The diagnosis came through her therapist, who specialized in women's issues and had recently attended training on autism in women. During a session where Simone described her elaborate systems for managing social interaction, the therapist paused and asked, "Has anyone ever evaluated you for autism?"

The question shocked Simone. She thought autism meant being unable to function socially or professionally. The assessment revealed that her apparent social competence came at enormous cost—cost she'd paid for decades without recognizing the transaction.

"Understanding I was autistic didn't change my capabilities. But it changed how I approached work. I stopped forcing myself into roles that required constant masking. I restructured my position to reduce social demands and increase analytic work. My job satisfaction increased and my 'depression' disappeared."

Case Study: Tamara's Educational Marathon

Tamara collected degrees—two bachelor's degrees, a master's, and a PhD—while struggling to maintain employment. Employers consistently praised her intelligence and technical skills but cited concerns about her "interpersonal communication" and "team fit."

"I never understood the feedback. I answered questions directly and honestly. I focused on producing high-quality work. I thought that's what mattered. But apparently, I was missing something about workplace culture that everyone else understood automatically."

Tamara experienced multiple job terminations, always during probationary periods. The pattern confused her. She performed the job tasks competently, but supervisors said she wasn't the "right fit" for the team.

"I started thinking I was unemployable despite my education. I went back to school repeatedly because academic environments made more sense to me than workplace cultures. But eventually I had to work, and the same problems kept appearing."

At 43, a career counselor suggested autism assessment. The evaluation confirmed what Tamara had never considered: she was autistic, and her workplace struggles stemmed from a mismatch between her processing style and typical workplace social expectations.

"The diagnosis explained why I could excel academically but struggle professionally. School had clear expectations and measurable outcomes. Workplace success required navigating ambiguous social norms and building relationships through small talk. I could learn information easily but couldn't intuit social rules."

Tamara now works as an independent researcher, controlling her work environment and client interactions. She succeeds by designing her professional life around her strengths rather than trying to force herself into traditional employment structures.

Case Study: Aisha's Therapy Odyssey

Aisha spent 15 years in various forms of therapy before receiving an autism diagnosis. She saw psychologists, psychiatrists, counselors, and social workers. She tried cognitive-behavioral therapy, dialectical behavior therapy, psychodynamic therapy, and medication management. Nothing produced lasting improvement.

"Every therapist identified different problems. One said I had attachment issues from childhood. Another focused on negative thought patterns. A third worked on emotional regulation. The interventions helped temporarily, but my core struggles persisted."

Aisha worked as a social worker—a choice that surprised her assessor. "People assume autistic people can't work in helping professions. But I was drawn to structured therapeutic approaches. One-on-one client work in a predictable format suited me. The difficulties came from office politics and team dynamics."

Her breakthrough came through a colleague who was also autistic. This colleague recognized similar patterns in Aisha's experiences and suggested she investigate autism in women. The formal assessment revealed what years of therapy had missed.

"The diagnosis reframed my entire therapeutic history. I hadn't been resistant to treatment or failing at recovery. I'd been trying to fix problems I didn't actually have while ignoring the real issue—that I was autistic and trying to function as neurotypical."

24

Aisha now works with an autism-informed therapist who focuses on developing sustainable strategies rather than trying to change fundamental aspects of how she processes the world. Her mental health has improved significantly.

Case Study: Nina's Creative Compensation

Nina worked as a professional photographer, a career that allowed her to pursue her intense interest in visual composition while limiting extensive social interaction. Clients appreciated her artistic vision and attention to detail. They had no idea she spent hours preparing for each client interaction, scripting conversations and anticipating possible scenarios.

"Photography attracted me because I could communicate through images rather than words. The technical aspects made sense to me. But the client management part required enormous effort. I created templates for every type of client interaction. I practiced my expressions in the mirror before shoots."

Nina experienced what she called "crashes"—periods where she couldn't function after intensive social periods like wedding season. She would spend weeks in near-isolation, unable to work or maintain basic self-care. Doctors diagnosed depression and prescribed medication that didn't help.

"I couldn't explain why I would be fine for months then suddenly unable to leave my house. It didn't follow the pattern of seasonal depression or major depressive episodes. Something else was happening."

At 36, Nina watched a documentary about autism in women. She recognized herself immediately and pursued assessment. The diagnosis explained her crashes as autistic burnout—the result of extended masking without adequate recovery time.

"Understanding autism changed my business model. I now limit the number of client interactions per month. I build in recovery time after social events. I communicate my needs more directly. My crashes became less frequent and less severe because I stopped pushing myself past sustainable limits."

Rewriting Your Life Story Through an Autism Lens

Receiving an autism diagnosis in adulthood forces a review of your entire life history. Experiences that seemed random or attributable to personal failure suddenly form a coherent pattern. The diagnosis provides a new interpretive framework.

You review childhood memories through this lens. The teacher who said you were "in your own world"—she was describing autism. The intense loneliness despite having friends—that reflected the exhaustion of constant social translation. The meltdowns at home after school—those were autistic burnout responses to overstimulation.

Adolescent struggles make new sense. The complete confusion about social hierarchies and unwritten rules wasn't stupidity. The difficulty maintaining friendships despite genuine care wasn't personal failing. The need for extensive alone time wasn't antisocial behavior. All of it reflected autistic traits you didn't have language to describe.

Adult patterns clarify. The serial job changes weren't lack of commitment. The difficulty with romantic relationships wasn't emotional unavailability. The exhaustion that seemed disproportionate to your activities wasn't weakness. Everything had an explanation—you were autistic, living in a world designed for a different neurotype.

This rewriting process produces complex emotions. Relief mixes with grief. You understand yourself better, but you also mourn the decades spent blaming yourself for struggles that weren't your fault. You feel validated, but you also feel angry that no one recognized this earlier.

Processing Grief, Relief, and Validation Simultaneously

The Relief Component

Most late-diagnosed autistic women describe profound relief upon diagnosis. For the first time, their experiences make sense. They're not broken or defective. They're not failing at being human. They have a neurological difference that explains their struggles.

This relief often arrives with tears. The release of decades of self-blame, the validation of experiences others dismissed, the acknowledgment that yes, this has been extraordinarily difficult—all of these produce overwhelming emotional responses.

"I cried for three days after my diagnosis," says Rachel, diagnosed at 41. "Not sad tears. Relief tears. I finally understood why everything had been so hard. I wasn't crazy. I wasn't making it up. I was autistic, and autism explained everything."

The Grief Component

Alongside relief comes grief for lost time and missed opportunities. You grieve for the child who struggled without support. You grieve for the teenager who blamed herself for social difficulties. You grieve for the young adult who pushed herself into burnout repeatedly without understanding why.

You grieve for relationships that failed because you didn't understand your own needs. You grieve for career opportunities you couldn't pursue because they required unsustainable masking. You grieve for the decades spent thinking something was wrong with you when actually something was wrong with the system that failed to recognize you.

This grief requires processing. You might feel angry at parents, teachers, or clinicians who missed the signs. You might feel frustrated with yourself for not recognizing it sooner. These emotions are legitimate and deserve acknowledgment.

The Validation Component

Validation might be the most powerful aspect of late diagnosis. Someone with expertise has confirmed that yes, your struggles were real. Yes, social interaction really is harder for you than for neurotypical people. Yes, sensory experiences really are overwhelming. Yes, the exhaustion has a legitimate cause.

For women who have been told repeatedly that they're too sensitive, too difficult, too emotional, or trying too hard—for women who have been gaslit about their own experiences for decades—this validation matters enormously.

"My whole life, people told me I was making things harder than they needed to be," says Jennifer, diagnosed at 38. "The diagnosis gave me permission to say, 'No, things actually are harder for me, and that's not my fault.' That permission changed everything."

Telling (or Not Telling) Others

The Disclosure Decision

Receiving an autism diagnosis creates an immediate question: who should know? The answer differs for each person and each relationship. Some factors to consider when deciding about disclosure:

Safety represents the primary consideration. Will disclosure put you at risk for discrimination, rejection, or harm? Unfortunately, autism stigma persists, and not all environments provide safety for disclosure.

Benefit to the relationship also matters. Will disclosure improve understanding and connection? For close relationships where you want deeper authenticity, disclosure might strengthen bonds. For distant or temporary relationships, disclosure might be unnecessary.

Need for accommodation represents another factor. If you need workplace accommodations or support from family members, disclosure becomes more necessary. You can't receive autism-specific support without explaining why you need it.

Disclosure Strategies for Different Contexts

Family disclosure often proves most emotionally complex. Parents may respond defensively, feeling blamed for missing the signs. Siblings might struggle to reconcile this new information with their established understanding of you. Extended family may dismiss the diagnosis entirely.

Strategies that help include providing information about autism in women, emphasizing that late diagnosis is common, and explaining how the diagnosis helps you understand yourself better. Give family members time to process. Their initial reactions may not represent their long-term response.

Workplace disclosure requires careful consideration of your legal protections and company culture. In the United States, the Americans with Disabilities Act protects against discrimination but only if you disclose. However, disclosure doesn't guarantee understanding or accommodation.

You might disclose to Human Resources officially while telling your direct supervisor informally. You might disclose only specific needs without mentioning autism. You might pursue accommodations through a doctor's note without personal disclosure. Each approach carries different risks and benefits.

Friend disclosure often feels less fraught than family or workplace disclosure. Close friends usually want to understand you better, and disclosure can deepen these relationships. You might disclose gradually, testing responses before sharing more extensively.

When Disclosure Goes Wrong

Not all disclosure experiences go well. Some people respond with dismissal: "Everyone feels that way sometimes." "You don't seem autistic." "Are you sure? You seem so normal." These responses invalidate your experience and reflect others' ignorance about autism.

Some respond with awkwardness or distancing. They don't know how to interact with you now that they have this information. The relationship becomes strained or ends entirely.

Some respond with infantilization, suddenly treating you as less competent than before disclosure. They offer unwanted help or make assumptions about your limitations.

These responses hurt, but they reveal more about the other person's understanding of autism than about you. Their reaction doesn't invalidate your diagnosis or your experience.

When Disclosure Goes Right

Positive disclosure experiences often involve the other person listening carefully, asking thoughtful questions, and expressing desire to understand and support you better. They might say things like:

"Thank you for trusting me with this information."

"How can I support you?"

"That explains some things I'd noticed but didn't understand."

"I'm glad you finally have an explanation for what you've been experiencing."

These responses validate your experience and strengthen the relationship. They demonstrate that disclosure to understanding people can create deeper connection rather than distance.

A New Beginning

Late diagnosis represents not an ending but a beginning. You're not late to the party—you've been at the party all along, just without understanding the music that's been playing. Now you have the sheet music, and everything makes more sense.

The diagnosis provides a foundation for building a life that works with your neurology rather than against it. The subsequent chapters will explore what this looks like practically: understanding your specific autistic profile, developing sustainable workplace strategies, and ultimately thriving rather than just surviving.

You've spent decades adapting to a neurotypical world without recognition of the effort required. Now you can begin making conscious choices about how much adaptation serves you and when to instead advocate for environmental changes that accommodate your needs. The diagnosis marks the transition from unconscious masking to conscious choice about how you want to move through the world.

A New Chapter Ahead

The women in these case studies share a common experience: diagnosis provided explanation but not immediate solution. Understanding you're autistic doesn't automatically eliminate struggles. But it does provide a framework for addressing those struggles more effectively.

You now face different questions than before diagnosis. Instead of asking "What's wrong with me?" you can ask "What accommodations would help me?" Instead of wondering why you're failing at things others find easy, you can recognize that you're succeeding at something extraordinarily difficult—functioning in a world designed for a different neurology.

The following chapters will build on this foundation, exploring the specific ways autism manifests in professional women and developing concrete strategies for sustainable success. The exhaustion of masking doesn't disappear with diagnosis, but understanding its source creates possibilities for change that didn't exist before.

Key Takeaways

Diagnostic Barriers

- Male-centric diagnostic criteria miss female presentations of autism

- Intensive social camouflaging hides traits that would trigger diagnosis

- Intelligence and cognitive compensation mask difficulties while creating exhaustion

- Current diagnostic tools often fail to detect autism in women who have learned to mask effectively

Common Misdiagnoses

- Anxiety and depression appear frequently but represent consequences rather than primary conditions

- Borderline personality disorder shares surface similarities but differs fundamentally in cause

- ADHD commonly coexists with autism but can also mask it when diagnosed alone

- Multiple incorrect diagnoses across decades create therapeutic frustration

The Assessment Process

- Self-recognition through online communities often precedes formal diagnosis

- Formal assessment requires finding clinicians trained in adult autism, particularly in women

- Standard assessment tools may miss masked presentations

- Self-diagnosis holds validity given systemic barriers to formal assessment

Processing the Diagnosis

- Relief, grief, and validation occur simultaneously

- Life history requires reinterpretation through the autism framework

- Disclosure decisions require careful consideration of context and safety

- Understanding autism creates foundation for different choices going forward

Chapter 3: The Female Autism Phenotype

The clinical portrait of autism—the one that appears in diagnostic manuals and medical textbooks—describes a specific presentation. This portrait emerged from decades of research conducted primarily with boys and men. But autism manifests differently across individuals, and systematic differences appear between typical male and female presentations. Understanding these differences matters because diagnostic and support systems built around male presentations systematically miss and underserve autistic women.

The female autism phenotype refers to the collection of characteristics commonly observed in autistic women and girls that differ from or appear less obviously than the characteristics emphasized in standard diagnostic criteria. This doesn't mean female autism represents a completely different condition. The core features remain—differences in social communication, sensory processing, and patterns of behavior and interest. But the specific manifestations of these features often differ.

How Autism Presents Differently in Professional Women

Social Motivation and Friendship

Standard autism descriptions emphasize lack of social interest. The stereotypical autistic person supposedly prefers solitude and shows little motivation for social connection. This description fits some autistic people but misses many autistic women entirely.

Most autistic women desperately want friendships. They observe their peers forming easy connections and yearn for similar relationships. The difficulty lies not in motivation but in execution. They want to connect but struggle with the mechanics of connection—the subtle timing of conversation, the unspoken rules governing intimacy, the mysterious process through which acquaintanceships deepen into friendships.

This pattern confuses clinicians who expect autistic people to lack social interest. They see a woman who tries hard socially and conclude she can't be autistic. They miss that the trying itself—the conscious, effortful attempting to do what neurotypical people accomplish automatically—indicates the core difference.

Gabrielle, a 35-year-old attorney, describes this experience: "I wanted friends desperately as a child. I studied how the popular girls interacted. I practiced their gestures and phrases. I tried everything to fit in. But I always felt like I was following a script I'd memorized rather than responding naturally. The effort exhausted me, and I never quite got it right. Clinicians saw my social efforts and assumed I couldn't be autistic. They didn't understand that my efforts proved the point—I had to work consciously at what others did naturally."

Camouflaging Through Imitation

Autistic women typically develop more sophisticated camouflaging strategies than autistic men. They observe social situations carefully and imitate behaviors they see working for others. This imitation can become remarkably detailed—copying specific phrases, facial expressions, gestures, and even clothing choices.

The imitation works superficially. The woman appears socially competent. She makes appropriate eye contact, produces suitable small talk, and navigates basic social situations without obvious difficulty. But the performance requires constant attention and exhausts her cognitive resources.

This camouflaging operates differently from conscious acting. Many autistic women can't articulate exactly what they're copying. The process becomes semi-automatic after years of practice. They've internalized thousands of social algorithms: If someone says this, respond with that. If you're in this type of situation, adopt this demeanor. But the algorithms remain algorithms—learned procedures rather than intuitive responses.

Relationship Patterns

Autistic women's friendships often show characteristic patterns. They may maintain one or two very close friendships while finding larger friend groups overwhelming. They might form intense bonds quickly but struggle to maintain multiple relationships simultaneously. They often prefer structured activities over unstructured social time.

Professional autistic women frequently report that work relationships feel easier than personal friendships. Work provides structure, clear roles, and defined purposes for interaction. Personal friendships require navigating ambiguous expectations and maintaining connection without clear purpose or schedule. The structure of work relationships reduces some of the difficulties that make personal relationships challenging.

Romantic relationships present their own challenges. Many autistic women report difficulties reading romantic interest, understanding dating conventions, and navigating the progression from dating to commitment. They might miss subtle flirting, interpret friendly behavior as romantic interest, or fail to recognize when someone is pursuing them romantically.

Special Interests as Career Foundations

Moving Beyond Trains and Dinosaurs

The stereotype of autistic special interests focuses on topics like trains, dinosaurs, or computers. These interests do appear among some autistic people. But autistic women's interests often focus on topics considered typical for women—animals, books, psychology, social justice, specific historical periods, or creative pursuits.

The difference lies not in the topic but in the intensity. The autistic woman doesn't just enjoy reading; she reads obsessively, consumes entire genres, and remembers extensive details about books and authors. She doesn't just like animals; she learns everything available about a specific species, advocates for animal welfare, and structures her life around animal care. She doesn't casually follow a social cause; she researches it extensively, develops detailed understanding, and dedicates significant time to advocacy.

This intensity often goes unrecognized as autistic because the interests themselves appear typical. A girl who reads constantly is just a bookworm. A woman dedicated to social justice is just passionate. The intensity that would raise concerns if focused on unusual topics gets normalized when focused on acceptable ones.

Special Interests as Career Paths

Many autistic women build successful careers around their special interests. The intense focus and extensive knowledge that characterize special interests become professional assets. The woman turns her encyclopedic knowledge of literature into work as an editor or librarian. She transforms her fascination with psychology into a counseling career. She builds her animal passion into veterinary medicine or wildlife biology.

This career alignment provides significant advantages. Work that connects to special interests feels intrinsically motivating rather than draining. The woman brings genuine enthusiasm and deep expertise to her profession. She might work longer hours without resentment because the work itself engages her interest rather than just providing income.

Dr. Vivian Chen, diagnosed at 42, built a career in molecular biology around her childhood fascination with cellular processes: "My parents thought I would outgrow my obsession with cells. In fifth grade, I would draw cellular diagrams for fun. I read college-level biology textbooks. I watched documentaries about microscopy repeatedly. Most people thought it was weird that a little girl cared so much about organelles."

"But I never outgrew it. I built my entire career on that early interest. My colleagues see dedication and passion. They don't realize I'm still that girl obsessed with cells—I just found a way to make it professionally viable."

Interest Cycling and Career Changes

Some autistic women experience interest cycling—periods of intense fascination with one topic followed by a shift to a different focus. This pattern can create career instability. The woman pursues a career aligned with one interest, then loses motivation when her interest shifts.

Understanding this pattern helps distinguish between restlessness or lack of commitment (common interpretations) and a neurological characteristic of how interests operate for some autistic people. The woman isn't failing at career stability—she's following the natural rhythm of her interest patterns.

Not all autistic women experience interest cycling. Some maintain the same special interests across their entire lives. But recognizing cycling as one possible pattern helps explain career paths that might otherwise appear scattered or unfocused.

Social Mimicry and Advanced Compensation Strategies

The Observation Process

Many autistic women describe spending their childhoods observing peers intensely. They watched how other girls interacted, noting patterns and rules. They studied facial expressions, body language, conversation timing, and social hierarchies. This observation represented active learning rather than passive watching.

The observation extended beyond conscious analysis. These women absorbed behavioral patterns at a detailed level, noticing micro-expressions, subtle tone shifts, and unspoken social dynamics. This absorption happened alongside explicit rule-learning, creating multiple layers of learned social behavior.

Naomi, diagnosed at 39, recalls her elementary school years: "I had a notebook where I wrote down social rules I'd figured out. 'When someone shows you something, say something nice about it.' 'If someone looks sad, ask if they're okay.' 'Don't talk about your interests unless someone asks.' I treated social interaction like a subject I needed to study, because that's what it was for me."

Developing Personas

Some autistic women develop distinct personas for different contexts. The work persona differs from the home persona. The persona for close friends differs from the persona for acquaintances. Each persona represents a set of behaviors, speech patterns, and interaction styles tailored to specific social contexts.

This persona-shifting goes beyond normal social adjustment. Everyone modifies their behavior somewhat across contexts. But the autistic woman's personas often feel like completely different characters rather than variations on her authentic self. Maintaining these distinct personas requires significant cognitive effort and can create identity confusion—which version represents the real self?

The professional persona particularly requires maintenance. The woman develops a work character who appears confident, socially competent, and professionally appropriate. This character might bear little resemblance to how she experiences herself internally. The gap between performance and internal experience creates a profound sense of disconnection.

Scripting and Its Limitations

Scripts provide another compensation strategy. The autistic woman memorizes appropriate responses for common situations: responses to "How are you?", appropriate compliments, sympathy expressions for bad news, enthusiasm expressions for good news. These scripts function like a phrasebook for social interaction.

Scripts work well for predictable situations. But they fail when situations deviate from expected patterns. Someone responds unexpectedly to a scripted opener. A conversation takes an unusual turn. The social context changes mid-interaction. In these moments, the woman must attempt real-time social processing—exactly the skill that scripts were designed to compensate for.

The script failure often reveals the underlying difficulty. The woman who appeared socially competent suddenly seems awkward or confused. She might fall silent, provide an inappropriate response, or resort to a script that doesn't fit the situation. These moments of mask-slippage can trigger anxiety about being "found out" as socially incompetent.

Case Study: Isabella's Chameleon Mastery

Isabella worked in public relations, a field requiring constant social interaction and relationship management. She excelled at her job, winning industry awards and managing high-profile clients. No one suspected she was autistic—including Isabella herself until age 40.

"I built my career on my ability to read people and adapt my communication style. I thought this was just good professional practice. I didn't realize I was compensating for autism by consciously doing what others did intuitively."

Isabella developed extensive systems for managing client relationships. She maintained detailed files on each client documenting their communication preferences, personal interests, family information, and interaction history. Before meetings, she reviewed these files and planned conversation topics. She created templates for different types of client interactions and practiced them before important calls.

"My colleagues thought I was incredibly organized. They didn't understand that without those systems, I couldn't function. I needed external structure to manage social relationships because I couldn't rely on social intuition."

The success of Isabella's compensation strategies prevented autism recognition for decades. She appeared hyper-competent socially—the opposite of autistic stereotypes. The diagnosis came only after burnout forced her to take medical leave and a perceptive therapist recognized masking behaviors in her descriptions of work processes.

Case Study: Yuki's Academic Success and Social Struggle

Yuki excelled academically throughout her life, earning a PhD in history and securing a faculty position at a research university. Her scholarship received recognition, and she earned tenure at a young age. But her personal life remained a source of pain and confusion.

"I could analyze historical social structures brilliantly. I could write about political movements and cultural shifts. But I couldn't navigate my own social world. The contradiction confused everyone, including me."

Yuki's special interest in history became her professional foundation. She could focus intensely on research for hours without fatigue. The solitary nature of scholarship suited her. The difficulties arose from the social aspects of academic life—faculty meetings, conferences, committee work, and departmental politics.

"I understood historical people better than contemporary ones. Historical social interaction followed documented patterns I could study. Contemporary social interaction required real-time processing I struggled with."

Yuki masked her social difficulties through scripts and avoidance. She memorized appropriate academic small talk. She limited conference attendance. She declined social invitations citing research deadlines. These strategies worked until the tenure process demanded increased social presence and collegiality.

"The tenure review explicitly mentioned concerns about my 'interpersonal skills' despite my excellent research record. That's when I sought evaluation, wondering if I had social anxiety. The assessment revealed autism, not anxiety disorder."

Case Study: Destiny's Corporate Code-Switching

Destiny built a successful career in corporate finance, a field dominated by men and characterized by aggressive communication styles. As a Black autistic woman, she developed extraordinarily complex masking strategies that addressed both neurotype and racial dynamics.

"I had to translate three ways simultaneously. I translated between my autistic and neurotypical communication styles. I translated between my cultural background and corporate white culture. I navigated being a woman in male-dominated spaces. The cognitive load was immense."

Destiny developed what she calls her "corporate persona"—a carefully constructed professional identity that masked both her autism and aspects of her cultural identity. She modified her speech patterns, suppressed stimming, and adopted communication styles that signaled corporate competence.

"I watched successful people obsessively. I studied how they spoke in meetings, how they handled disagreements, how they projected confidence. I created detailed rules for myself about professional behavior. I thought everyone did this level of planning."

The diagnosis at age 37 reframed Destiny's experiences. The exhaustion she attributed to racism and sexism—real factors she definitely encountered—also reflected autism-related masking. Understanding the autism piece helped her distinguish which struggles stemmed from which source and develop more targeted coping strategies.

"Racism and sexism require one set of responses. Autism-related challenges require different responses. Understanding I was managing all three simultaneously helped me stop blaming myself for the exhaustion."

Sensory Sensitivities That Hide in Plain Sight

Socially Acceptable Sensory Preferences

Autistic sensory sensitivities in women often manifest as strong preferences that seem quirky but not pathological. The woman has favorite textures and avoids others. She's "picky" about food. She prefers certain types of lighting. She gets headaches easily. These traits exist on a spectrum where they can be dismissed as preferences rather than recognized as sensory processing differences.

The distinction matters because preferences suggest choice while sensory processing differences indicate neurological variation. The woman doesn't prefer soft fabrics as an aesthetic choice—her nervous system processes scratchy textures as painful stimuli. She doesn't avoid certain foods to be difficult—specific tastes or textures trigger overwhelming sensory responses.

Professional environments create multiple sensory challenges. Fluorescent lighting, background noise, temperature regulation, strong scents, and physical contact all present potential difficulties. The autistic woman who masks often suppresses her reactions to these stimuli, enduring sensory distress without outward indication.

Melissa, a 33-year-old teacher, describes her sensory experience: "The classroom lighting hurt my eyes, but I thought everyone experienced this. The noise level triggered physical pain, but I assumed I needed to toughen up. The scratchy dress clothes required for professionalism made my skin crawl, but I told myself I was being too sensitive. I normalized significant sensory distress because I didn't realize my experiences differed from others'."

Sensory-Seeking vs. Sensory-Avoiding

Some autistic individuals avoid sensory input while others seek it. Many women combine both patterns—avoiding some sensory experiences while seeking others. The woman might hate loud environments but love deep pressure. She might avoid bright lights but seek out intense visual stimulation through detailed artwork. She might be oversensitive to touch in some contexts but crave firm hugs.

This mixed pattern sometimes prevents recognition of sensory processing differences. Clinicians expect consistent hyper- or hypo-sensitivity. The woman who shows both patterns might appear inconsistent rather than showing the complex sensory profile common in autism.

Sensory Overload and Shutdown

When sensory input exceeds processing capacity, autistic people experience overload. For women who mask, this overload often happens internally without obvious external signs. The woman continues appearing professional while experiencing internal sensory crisis.

Extended overload leads to shutdown—a state where the person's capacity for interaction, communication, and function decreases dramatically. The woman who masks might push through initial overload, but shutdown eventually becomes unavoidable. She reaches home and collapses, unable to speak, interact, or manage basic tasks.

This pattern creates confusion for romantic partners and family members. The woman appears fine at work but non-functional at home. Partners sometimes interpret this as the woman saving her "good" behavior for work and treating family members poorly. Understanding that she's masking at work and experiencing shutdown at home reframes the dynamic.

Executive Function Challenges Masked by Over-Preparation

The Planning Paradox

Executive function encompasses planning, organization, task initiation, time management, and cognitive flexibility. Many autistic adults struggle with these skills. But autistic women often hide executive function challenges through extensive preparation and systems.

The woman creates detailed schedules, elaborate checklists, and extensive backup plans. She appears hyper-organized. Others see someone with exceptional executive function. They miss that the elaborate systems exist precisely because her executive function struggles without explicit external structure.

This paradox creates problems when systems fail. Life inevitably includes situations that resist planning—emergencies, unexpected changes, ambiguous tasks. When situations exceed her preparation capacity, the woman's underlying executive function challenges become visible. But by then, she's established a reputation for competence that makes the struggles seem like temporary lapses rather than consistent patterns.

Time Management and Time Blindness

Many autistic people experience time blindness—difficulty estimating time passage and managing time-based tasks. The woman who masks often compensates by arriving excessively early, setting multiple alarms, and building extensive buffers into her schedule.

These compensations hide the time blindness while creating their own problems. The woman who arrives 30 minutes early to avoid being late spends significant time waiting. The woman who sets eight alarms experiences fragmented sleep. The woman who blocks out twice as much time as needed for tasks sacrifices efficiency for certainty.

Professional environments punish lateness but rarely acknowledge the cost of extreme punctuality achieved through compensatory strategies. The autistic woman who arrives early and prepared appears ideal. No one sees the anxiety and effort required to achieve this appearance.

Cognitive Flexibility and Change Management

Cognitive flexibility—the ability to shift between tasks, adapt to changing situations, and handle unexpected developments—often challenges autistic people. Changes in routine, unexpected developments, and ambiguous situations all require cognitive flexibility.

The masking autistic woman typically responds to this challenge by minimizing change whenever possible. She develops rigid routines and becomes distressed when they're disrupted. But she hides this distress, forcing herself through changes while experiencing internal turmoil.

Professional life inevitably includes change—new projects, shifting priorities, organizational restructures. The woman who struggles with cognitive flexibility but masks this struggle appears adaptable while experiencing significant stress from each change.

Case Study: Rhiannon's System Dependency

Rhiannon worked as a project manager, a role requiring extensive organizational skills and ability to coordinate multiple moving parts. She excelled, consistently delivering projects on time and within budget. Her systematic approach impressed colleagues and supervisors.

"I had systems for everything. Color-coded calendars. Detailed project templates. Checklists within checklists. Regular check-in schedules. Everything structured and documented."

What colleagues saw as exceptional organization actually represented compensation for executive function challenges. Without elaborate systems, Rhiannon struggled with basic tasks. She couldn't estimate time accurately. She forgot tasks unless they appeared on lists. She couldn't prioritize without explicit decision frameworks.

"If someone asked me to do something without my established systems, I would panic. Take a simple question like 'Can you handle this?' I couldn't answer without running through my entire task list, checking my calendar, and calculating how long the new task would take. What others did intuitively—quick mental checks of capacity—required extensive conscious processing for me."

The limitations became apparent when Rhiannon's company restructured, eliminating established workflows and implementing new systems. The change disrupted all of her compensatory structures. Without her systems, her executive function difficulties became visible.

"I went from star performer to struggling employee within weeks. Management thought I'd become suddenly incompetent. Actually, they'd removed the supports that enabled my competence."

Case Study: Anya's Preparation Intensity

Anya worked as a conference presenter, conducting training workshops for professional organizations. She received excellent evaluations, with participants praising her clear presentations and expertise. No one knew she spent 40 hours preparing for each 2-hour workshop.

"For every presentation, I created detailed scripts. I practiced repeatedly, timing every section. I anticipated every possible question and prepared responses. I visited venues early to understand the space. I created backup plans for technology failures, participant reactions, and schedule changes."

This extensive preparation produced excellent presentations but required unsustainable effort. Anya could conduct four workshops per month before exhaustion forced her to decline additional bookings. Colleagues who could deliver workshops with minimal preparation couldn't understand her limitations.

"People assumed I was perfectionistic or anxious. Actually, I needed that preparation because I couldn't improvise. If something unexpected happened during a workshop, I struggled. The over-preparation was compensating for executive function challenges—

specifically, difficulty with cognitive flexibility and real-time problem-solving."

Understanding her autism helped Anya restructure her business. She reduced the number of workshops she offered, built in more recovery time, and developed modular presentation components that reduced preparation requirements. Her income decreased, but sustainability improved.

The High IQ Paradox: Intelligence as Camouflage

Cognitive Compensation Strategies

Higher cognitive ability provides autistic women with tools for compensating. They can analyze social situations logically, creating rules and frameworks that substitute for intuitive understanding. They can memorize scripts and study patterns. They can construct elaborate systems that manage their executive function challenges.

This compensation works but requires significant cognitive resources. The intelligent autistic woman succeeds at appearing neurotypical through continuous conscious effort. She analyzes everything that neurotypical people process automatically. The mental calculation never stops.

The paradox: the same intelligence that enables compensation also masks the need for support. The woman appears competent, so no one recognizes her struggles. By the time her compensation strategies fail, she's often in crisis, and people around her find the sudden decline confusing because they never saw the effort maintaining apparent competence.

Academic Success and Autism Oversight

Schools identify autism more readily in students who struggle academically. The autistic girl who excels academically often escapes notice, even when showing clear social and sensory difficulties. Intelligence becomes camouflage that prevents recognition of the autism underneath.

Dr. Patel, diagnosed at 48 after a distinguished academic career, reflects on this dynamic: "I was a straight-A student. Teachers overlooked my social isolation and sensory sensitivities because I performed well academically. No one connected my difficulties to autism because I succeeded at school tasks."

This pattern persists into professional life. The woman who produces excellent work receives promotions and recognition. Her social struggles get attributed to introversion or interpersonal style rather than recognized as autism-related challenges.

The Collapse Point

Compensation through intelligence works until it doesn't. The woman maintains apparent competence through adolescence, through college, through early career. Then something shifts—increased responsibility, life transitions, accumulated exhaustion—and the compensation strategies fail.

This collapse often confuses everyone, including the woman herself. She's been competent for decades. Why is everything suddenly falling apart? The answer: the compensation was never effortless, and the cumulative strain eventually exceeded capacity.

Understanding autism explains the collapse. It wasn't sudden failure but delayed recognition of ongoing struggle. The intelligence that enabled years of compensation couldn't indefinitely sustain the mismatch between her neurology and environmental demands.

Understanding Your Unique Autistic Profile

Individual Variation Within Autism

Autism manifests uniquely in each person. Two autistic women may share diagnostic criteria while showing completely different profiles. One might excel at verbal communication but struggle with sensory processing. Another might have significant verbal challenges but excellent visual-spatial abilities. A third might experience intense sensory sensitivities but fewer social difficulties.

Understanding your personal profile requires self-observation and often external assessment. What specific situations trigger struggle? What skills come naturally versus requiring conscious effort? Which autistic characteristics appear prominently versus minimally in your experience?

Strength-Challenge Mapping

Creating a personal map of strengths and challenges helps with self-understanding and advocacy. This mapping goes beyond simple lists to examine patterns and contexts.

Pattern recognition represents a strength for many autistic people. You might excel at identifying trends, seeing connections, and solving puzzle-like problems. Understanding this strength helps you seek roles that utilize pattern recognition while building in supports for areas of challenge.

Detail orientation often appears as both strength and challenge. Noticing small details enhances quality control, editing, research, and analysis. But it can also make it difficult to see big pictures or let go of minor imperfections. Understanding this dual nature helps you leverage the strength while managing the challenge.

Sensory sensitivity creates challenges in many environments but can also enhance certain abilities. The woman sensitive to visual detail might excel at design, art, or data visualization. The woman with acute auditory processing might work effectively in music or audio engineering. Reframing sensory sensitivity as information processing difference rather than pure deficit opens possibilities.

Contextual Variation

Your autistic characteristics likely vary across contexts. You might function well in structured environments but struggle with ambiguous situations. You might manage one-on-one interactions effectively but find group dynamics overwhelming. You might handle routine tasks easily but experience significant difficulty with unexpected changes.

Recognizing contextual variation helps explain patterns that might otherwise seem contradictory. You're not inconsistent—your abilities reflect the interaction between your neurological processing and environmental demands. Understanding which contexts support your functioning and which create challenge allows for better decision-making about work environments, social engagements, and daily routines.

Moving Forward with Self-Understanding

Understanding the female autism phenotype provides language for experiences you've had your entire life. The social observation and mimicry, the sensory sensitivities framed as preferences, the executive function challenges hidden by elaborate systems, the intelligence used for constant compensation—these patterns describe your reality.

This understanding changes nothing about your neurology. You remain autistic with all the challenges and strengths that entails. But understanding creates new possibilities. You can stop blaming yourself for difficulties that stem from neurological difference. You can seek environments that accommodate rather than challenge your processing style. You can make conscious choices about when masking serves your purposes and when it extracts too high a price.

The autistic professional woman faces unique challenges—managing the double burden of gender expectations and neurological difference, navigating workplaces designed for neurotypical interaction patterns, and sustaining careers while managing the exhaustion of continuous masking. But understanding your specific profile provides the foundation for developing sustainable strategies that allow professional success without personal destruction.

Turning Understanding Into Action

The female autism phenotype describes common patterns, but you are not a collection of patterns—you're an individual with a unique constellation of characteristics, strengths, and challenges. The next chapters will build on this understanding, exploring how to create sustainable work situations, develop effective accommodations, and ultimately thrive professionally while honoring your authentic autistic self.

You've spent years or decades functioning in environments that didn't account for your neurological differences. Understanding those differences now provides the foundation for different choices— choices that prioritize sustainability over superhuman effort, that seek accommodation rather than constant adaptation, and that allow for success defined by thriving rather than just surviving.

Key Takeaways

Distinctive Presentation Patterns

- Autistic women typically show strong social motivation despite social difficulties

- Camouflaging through sophisticated imitation masks autistic traits while creating exhaustion

- Friendship and relationship patterns differ from stereotypical autism descriptions but reflect core social processing differences

Interest and Career Connections

- Special interests in autistic women often focus on socially typical topics, making them less recognizable as autistic

- Intensity of interest rather than topic distinguishes autistic special interests

- Many autistic women build successful careers around special interests, creating professional advantage

Compensation Strategies

- Intelligence enables complex compensation through rules, scripts, and conscious analysis

- Extensive preparation and elaborate systems mask executive function challenges

- Compensation success prevents autism recognition while creating unsustainable demands

Sensory and Cognitive Patterns

- Sensory sensitivities often appear as strong preferences rather than obvious processing differences

- Executive function challenges hide behind over-preparation and extensive systems

- Time blindness, difficulty with change, and cognitive flexibility challenges persist despite apparent adaptability

Individual Profiles

- Each autistic woman shows a unique profile of strengths and challenges

- Contextual variation in functioning reflects interaction between neurology and environment

- Understanding personal patterns enables better environmental choices and accommodation requests

Chapter 4: The Workplace Reality Check

Professional environments present themselves as meritocracies—work hard, produce results, advance your career. But this narrative assumes all workers start from the same baseline, process information similarly, and expend equivalent energy on work tasks. For the autistic professional woman, none of these assumptions hold true. She enters a workplace designed for neurotypical sensory processing, social interaction patterns, and communication styles. Success requires not just performing her job but simultaneously translating between her natural processing style and the expected neurotypical presentation.

The workplace reality check arrives when you realize that your exhaustion stems not from inadequacy but from operating in an environment that requires constant neurological translation. You're running two jobs simultaneously—the one you were hired for and the job of appearing neurotypical while doing it. This chapter examines the specific workplace challenges autistic women face and explores both survival strategies and paths toward actual thriving.

Open Office Plans and Sensory Assault

Modern workplace design trends toward open offices, collaborative spaces, and activity-based working. These environments claim to increase collaboration and creativity. For neurotypical workers, these spaces may achieve their goals. For autistic workers, they create constant sensory overload that prevents concentration and drains cognitive resources.

The Auditory Layer

Sound in open offices arrives from multiple sources simultaneously. Colleagues conduct phone conversations three feet away. Meetings happen in "huddle spaces" without sound barriers. Keyboards click. Heating systems hum. Doors open and close. Coffee machines gurgle. Each sound competes for your attention, fragmenting concentration into useless pieces.

Neurotypical workers filter irrelevant sounds automatically, focusing on their tasks while background noise fades. Autistic sensory processing often lacks this automatic filtering. All sounds register with similar intensity. You hear every conversation, every mechanical noise, every footstep. Your brain processes these sounds consciously rather than automatically, using cognitive resources that should be available for work.

The result? Work that should take two hours requires four because you're constantly interrupted by sounds you can't ignore. Tasks requiring deep concentration become nearly impossible. You might complete them by arriving early, staying late, or working from home—all strategies that extend your work hours while colleagues complete the same tasks during normal hours.

Visual Overstimulation

Fluorescent lighting flickers at frequencies some autistic people consciously perceive. The flicker creates visual strain, headaches, and difficulty focusing. Natural light varies in intensity, creating glare on computer screens. Colleagues move constantly in your peripheral vision. Visual clutter from open shelving and exposed storage creates constant low-level distraction.

Each visual stimulus requires processing. Your brain can't automatically filter movement in your peripheral vision the way neurotypical brains do. You see everything, process everything, and exhaust your visual processing capacity long before the workday ends.

Temperature and Tactile Sensitivities

Office climate control systems create temperature variations. One zone feels frigid while another feels stifling. You can't control your immediate environment because the thermostat serves an entire floor. Dress codes require specific fabrics or styles that might trigger tactile sensitivities. Office furniture creates pressure points or fails to provide adequate support.

These sensory challenges don't appear on performance reviews. Your supervisor doesn't see the migraine building from fluorescent lights or the distraction caused by constant background noise. They see only that you request headphones, seem distracted, or prefer working alone. The accommodations you need can be interpreted as antisocial behavior or lack of team spirit.

Case Study: Carmen's Corporate Cubicle to Open Office Disaster

Carmen worked as a financial analyst at a mid-sized firm. For eight years, she had a cubicle—not ideal, but manageable. The partial walls provided some sound dampening and visual barriers. She could concentrate, produce detailed analyses, and maintain her reputation as a top performer.

Then her company restructured, moving to an open office plan designed by a consultant who promised increased collaboration and innovation. Carmen's cubicle disappeared, replaced by a desk in a room containing 40 other people. No walls. No barriers. Pure sensory chaos.

"The first day in the new space, I felt my chest tighten within an hour. By lunch, I had a splitting headache. I couldn't concentrate on simple tasks. Numbers swam on my screen. I made calculation errors I'd never made before."

Carmen tried adaptation strategies. She wore headphones playing white noise. She positioned her monitor to minimize glare. She requested a desk in a corner, hoping for slight reduction in peripheral visual stimulation. Nothing helped sufficiently.

"My performance dropped immediately. Tasks that took me two hours now took six. I started making mistakes. My manager called me in to discuss my 'recent performance issues.' I tried to explain that the office environment made concentration impossible, but he said everyone else had adapted fine. He suggested I wasn't being 'flexible' enough."

Carmen wasn't diagnosed autistic at the time. She thought she was failing, that she lacked resilience or adaptability. After six months of declining performance, she accepted a severance package and left the company. Only later, after receiving an autism diagnosis, did she understand that her struggles reflected sensory processing differences, not personal failure.

She now works remotely for a different company, controlling her sensory environment and producing work at her previous high level. The open office didn't reveal incompetence—it revealed workplace design incompatible with her neurology.

Case Study: Becca's Battle with Buzzing Lights

Becca worked as a software developer. She loved coding—the logic, the problem-solving, the satisfaction of elegant solutions. But her office environment created constant distress that she hid for years before it became unsustainable.

The fluorescent lights in her office flickered at a frequency she could consciously perceive. "I tried to explain it to my manager. I said the lights flickered and it bothered me. He looked up and said, 'They're not flickering.' To him, they weren't. To me, they created a constant strobe effect that felt like someone was flashing a light in my face all day."

Becca developed chronic headaches. She started wearing sunglasses at her desk, which prompted comments from colleagues who joked about her "hangover glasses." She requested a desk lamp so she could turn off the overhead lights in her area, but the building facilities manager said individual lighting violated safety codes.

"I was spending 50% of my cognitive capacity managing sensory distress and 50% actually coding. My productivity dropped. I got feedback that I seemed 'checked out' during team meetings. I wasn't checked out—I was trying not to vomit from the sensory overload while also participating in discussions about software architecture."

After two years, Becca developed severe anxiety that her doctor initially attributed to work stress. Medication helped somewhat with the anxiety but didn't address the underlying sensory issues. She eventually requested reasonable accommodation under the Americans with Disabilities Act, providing medical documentation of her sensory sensitivities.

Her company relocated her to a different floor with LED lighting that didn't trigger the same response. Her headaches decreased. Her productivity recovered. Her anxiety symptoms improved significantly. The accommodation cost the company nothing beyond the administrative time to arrange the desk move. But Becca had suffered for two years before discovering she could request accommodation.

Unwritten Social Rules and Office Politics

Every workplace operates through both official policies and unofficial social norms. The employee handbook explains vacation procedures and sexual harassment policies. But the handbook doesn't explain that you should compliment your boss's new haircut, that you should attend happy hours even if they're officially optional, or that you should laugh at jokes you don't find funny.

These unwritten rules govern everything: how to disagree respectfully, when to speak in meetings, how to request help without appearing incompetent, when to work from home versus showing face time, how to decline social invitations without appearing unsociable. Neurotypical workers absorb these rules through observation and social intuition. Autistic workers must learn them explicitly, often through trial and error that can damage professional relationships.

The Compliment Economy

Workplace relationships operate partly through compliment exchange. Colleagues comment positively on each other's presentations, outfits, ideas, and weekend activities. These compliments serve social bonding functions separate from their literal content.

The autistic woman often struggles with this system. Should she compliment something she doesn't actually find impressive? Should she point out flaws in a colleague's reasoning when asked for feedback? If someone's presentation was genuinely mediocre, should she say so or offer praise anyway?

The neurotypical answer: offer praise for effort, positivity, or some aspect you can honestly compliment. The literal accuracy of the compliment matters less than the social function it serves. But this calculation requires recognizing the social function, something that doesn't come naturally to many autistic people.

Reading Between the Lines

Office communication relies heavily on implication and indirect speech. "Do you have a moment?" means "I need your time now for an unspecified duration." "Let me think about that" means "No, but I don't want to say no directly." "That's an interesting idea" might mean "That's a terrible idea but I'm being polite."

Neurotypical workers decode these implications automatically. Autistic workers often take statements literally, leading to miscommunication. You think you've been asked to consider whether you have a moment available and answer honestly: "Actually, I'm on a deadline." Your colleague interprets this as rudeness or unwillingness to help.

Learning to recognize and produce indirect communication requires explicit instruction and practice. Even then, it feels like using a translation guide rather than speaking naturally. The cognitive load of constant translation accumulates throughout the workday.

Office Politics and Coalition Building

Career advancement often depends not just on work quality but on relationship networks, perceived influence, and coalition membership. You need allies who advocate for you in promotion discussions. You need visibility with decision-makers. You need to be seen as "leadership material"—a vague concept involving social performance as much as actual capability.

Many autistic women struggle with office politics not from lack of ambition but from genuine confusion about the system. Who has actual influence versus official authority? How do you build alliances without appearing manipulative? What signals indicate that someone is blocking your advancement? The answers to these questions require reading subtle social cues and understanding power dynamics that aren't explicitly stated.

Case Study: Diane's Direct Communication Disaster

Diane worked in marketing, specifically in data analysis and campaign performance measurement. She excelled at quantitative analysis, identifying trends, and producing clear reports. Her analytical skills were excellent. Her political skills were non-existent.

During a team meeting, her manager presented a campaign strategy Diane immediately recognized as flawed. The target demographic analysis was incorrect, the messaging didn't align with the data, and the budget allocation was inefficient. Diane raised her hand and explained these problems in detail, providing specific data points and alternative approaches.

The room went silent. Her manager's face flushed. A senior colleague interjected with a vague positive comment about "exploring different perspectives." The meeting ended awkwardly.

"I thought I was being helpful. I had data showing the problems. Wasn't that what analysis was for—to improve decision-making? But apparently, I'd committed some social violation by publicly pointing out errors in my manager's strategy."

Later, a colleague explained that Diane should have raised concerns privately with her manager, phrased critiques as questions rather than statements, and offered praise before criticism. Diane had violated multiple unwritten rules: don't embarrass superiors publicly, don't appear arrogant about your expertise, maintain group harmony over accuracy.

"I understood the explicit rules about respectful workplace behavior. But these implicit rules about protecting egos and maintaining hierarchy even when accuracy suffers—those made no sense to me. Wasn't accurate data the point of hiring analysts?"

Diane's direct communication style damaged her career prospects. She received feedback about needing to develop "interpersonal skills" and "emotional intelligence." Her technical competence was never questioned, but her advancement stalled because she couldn't navigate the social dimensions of workplace hierarchy.

After receiving an autism diagnosis, Diane worked with a career coach to learn explicit strategies for workplace diplomacy. She developed scripts for delivering criticism diplomatically and rules for identifying when to speak versus when to stay silent. These learned skills helped, but they required constant conscious application.

Meeting Overload and Communication Challenges

Modern workplaces run on meetings. Status updates. Brainstorming sessions. Project check-ins. Team building. All-hands announcements. One-on-ones. Cross-functional collaboration. The meeting load expands to fill available time.

For neurotypical workers, meetings serve multiple functions: information exchange, social bonding, status signaling, collaborative thinking. Many neurotypical people find meetings energizing despite complaining about them. For autistic workers, meetings extract enormous energy while providing limited value.

Processing Time Delays

Autistic people often need processing time to formulate responses. Someone asks a question in a meeting. The neurotypical response arrives within seconds. The autistic person might need 30 seconds or a minute to process the question, access relevant information, and formulate an answer. By that time, the conversation has moved on.

This processing delay makes you appear slow, disengaged, or confused. You might have brilliant insights about an issue, but they arrive after the discussion has shifted to the next topic. Speaking up after the conversation has moved on feels awkward, so you stay silent. Your contributions go unrecognized, and your competence gets underestimated.

Sensory and Social Overload

Meetings combine social interaction with sensory challenges. You're monitoring multiple people's facial expressions, tone, and body language while processing verbal content. You're managing your own facial expressions and body language to appear engaged. You're filtering background noise, adjusting to lighting, and maintaining physical stillness despite the urge to stim.

All this happens simultaneously while you're expected to contribute intelligent thoughts about the meeting topic. The multitasking required exceeds your processing capacity. You might focus intensely on the content and miss social cues, or you might focus on social performance and miss content details.

Virtual Meeting Complications

Remote work introduced video meetings that create their own challenges. You must monitor your own video feed, adjusting camera angles and checking your appearance. You must watch multiple video squares showing other participants. Audio delays complicate turn-taking. The constant visual and social self-monitoring exhausts you differently than in-person meetings but equally thoroughly.

Case Study: Fatima's Meeting Marathon Breakdown

Fatima worked as a project coordinator for a consulting firm. Her job involved managing timelines, tracking deliverables, and communicating progress—tasks she handled well through email and project management software. But her company culture required constant meetings.

"I had meetings scheduled from 9 AM to 5 PM most days. Back-to-back 30-minute or hour-long blocks. Status updates. Client calls. Internal planning. Team building. I would finish the day having attended eight meetings but completed zero actual work."

Fatima adapted by working evenings and weekends to complete tasks she couldn't finish during meeting-filled days. Her work quality remained high, but her hours became unsustainable. She developed insomnia. She stopped exercising. Her relationships suffered.

"During meetings, I was performing. Maintaining appropriate facial expressions. Responding at appropriate times. Processing multiple people talking simultaneously. By the end of the day, I had no cognitive resources left for actual work. So I'd go home, rest for an hour, then work from 8 PM to midnight."

After two years, Fatima experienced what she now recognizes as autistic burnout. She couldn't maintain the pace anymore. Her performance dropped. She made errors. She called in sick frequently. Her manager addressed the absences in a performance review, noting that Fatima seemed "checked out" lately.

"I tried to explain that the meeting load was destroying my productivity. My manager said meetings were part of the job and everyone had to attend them. He suggested time management training, which was absurd—I didn't need time management skills. I needed fewer meetings."

Fatima ultimately left that position. She now works for a company with a "no meeting Wednesdays" policy and a culture that respects asynchronous communication. Her productivity increased. Her mental health improved. The problem wasn't Fatima's capacity—it was the meeting-intensive work environment.

The Energy Accounting Problem

You finish a workday and feel completely depleted. Your neurotypical colleagues head to happy hour or the gym. You go home and collapse. You might not manage dinner. Showering feels overwhelming. You need hours of complete silence and solitude before you can function again.

This exhaustion confuses people. You sat at a desk all day. You didn't do physical labor. Why are you so tired? The answer lies in energy accounting—the calculation of energy expended versus energy available.

The Masking Tax

Every hour you spend masking extracts energy. Forcing eye contact. Suppressing stims. Monitoring your facial expressions. Processing social cues consciously. Managing sensory input. All of this requires active cognitive effort that neurotypical workers don't expend.

Think of it this way: if neurotypical workers spend 100 energy units on their job tasks, you spend 60 units masking and 40 units on actual work. You're completing the same work but with fewer resources allocated to it. To produce comparable output, you must either work longer hours or be extraordinarily efficient with your limited task-focused energy.

Sensory Processing Overhead

Processing sensory input in overstimulating environments creates constant background drain. Imagine your brain as a computer running multiple programs. The neurotypical worker has browser tabs open for their work tasks. You have those same tabs plus 20 additional tabs running sensory processing programs. Your system runs slower because more resources are allocated to basic environmental processing.

Social Interaction Energy Cost

Social interactions that neurotypical workers find energizing or neutral deplete your resources. A five-minute chat by the coffee machine costs you energy that your neurotypical colleague recovers from that interaction. A lunch with colleagues that they find relaxing leaves you exhausted from managing conversation, reading social cues, and suppressing your discomfort with the restaurant's sensory environment.

Case Study: Priya's Invisible Energy Crisis

Priya worked as a research scientist. Lab work suited her perfectly—structured tasks, clear protocols, minimal social interaction. But her job also required teaching, attending departmental meetings, and supervising graduate students. These social and communication-heavy aspects drained her energy disproportionately.

"A day in the lab left me pleasantly tired, ready for evening activities. A day filled with meetings and teaching left me so depleted I could barely drive home safely. I would sit in my car in the parking garage for 30 minutes before I had enough energy to drive."

Priya tried explaining this pattern to her department chair, who dismissed it as introversion. "He said everyone finds social interaction tiring and I needed to manage my energy better. But this wasn't normal tiredness—it was complete cognitive depletion. I couldn't process language properly. I couldn't make simple decisions. I needed hours of recovery."

Priya started declining committee assignments and student mentorship opportunities. Her department chair noted this as a lack of service commitment in her annual review. When Priya tried to explain her energy limitations, he suggested she wasn't suited for academic life, which required balanced contributions across research, teaching, and service.

After receiving an autism diagnosis, Priya requested accommodation through her university's disability services office. She received reduced teaching loads and exemptions from some committee work, with her service contributions redirected to written reviews and remote participation options. Her productivity in research increased, and her overall wellbeing improved significantly.

"The accommodations weren't special treatment—they were adjustments that let me allocate my energy toward my actual strengths instead of draining it on activities that provided minimal value relative to their cost for me."

Performance Reviews That Miss the Mark

Annual performance reviews supposedly measure your contributions objectively. But they often emphasize social performance— teamwork, communication, leadership presence—as heavily as actual work output. The autistic woman who produces excellent work but struggles with office politics receives mixed reviews that hinder advancement.

The Teamwork Trap

Performance reviews often include ratings for "teamwork" or "collaboration." These categories supposedly measure your ability to work effectively with others. But they frequently measure your conformity to neurotypical social norms instead.

You might collaborate excellently through written communication, providing detailed feedback and supporting colleagues' projects. But you struggle with brainstorming sessions that require rapid-fire verbal contributions. Your performance review notes that you "could be more engaged in team discussions," missing that you contribute extensively through other channels.

Communication Style Bias

Reviews often penalize direct communication styles while rewarding indirect approaches. You state problems clearly and suggest solutions explicitly—this gets labeled as "too blunt" or "lacking diplomacy."

Your neurotypical colleague frames the same criticism as a question or suggestion—this gets labeled as "constructive feedback."

The content is identical. The social packaging differs. But the review treats packaging as equally important as content, putting you at a disadvantage for being straightforward.

Leadership Presence Mystification

Many reviews reference "leadership presence" or "executive presence" without defining these terms clearly. They involve social performance: projecting confidence, building consensus, inspiring others, navigating politics. These skills are learnable but don't come naturally to many autistic people.

You might lead effectively through clear planning, competent decision-making, and technical expertise. But without the social performance aspect, your leadership doesn't "read" as leadership to neurotypical evaluators.

Case Study: Natasha's Stellar Output, Mediocre Reviews

Natasha worked as a data scientist producing analyses that directly influenced company strategy. Her work was consistently excellent—thorough, accurate, insightful. But her performance reviews were mediocre.

"My technical ratings were always top tier. My 'collaboration' and 'communication' ratings were always marked as 'needs improvement.' These ratings balanced out to overall 'meets expectations' rather than 'exceeds expectations,' which I clearly did in my actual job performance."

Natasha excelled at solo analytical work. She communicated results clearly in writing. She responded promptly to questions and helped colleagues understand her analyses. But she didn't engage in casual office chat. She didn't attend many social events. She asked for clarity about ambiguous requests instead of reading between the lines.

"My manager said I needed to be 'more visible' and 'build relationships.' But I was already doing the work. What they wanted was the performance of sociability on top of the work."

After her autism diagnosis, Natasha requested a meeting with HR and her manager. She explained that her communication style reflected neurological difference, not attitude problems. She provided medical documentation supporting accommodation requests: clear written feedback on her actual work performance, separation of social expectations from technical performance evaluation, and recognition that her preferred communication style through written channels was legitimate professional communication.

Her subsequent review acknowledged her technical excellence without penalizing her communication style. Her career advancement improved once her actual contributions were properly recognized.

Working from Home as Accidental Accommodation

The COVID-19 pandemic forced many workplaces into remote arrangements. For autistic women, this shift often revealed something striking: given control over their sensory environment and communication methods, their performance improved dramatically while their exhaustion decreased.

Sensory Control

Working from home lets you control lighting, temperature, sound, and other sensory variables. You use lamps instead of fluorescent lights. You set the temperature to your preference. You control background noise. You wear comfortable clothes regardless of dress codes.

These adjustments aren't luxuries—they're accommodations that let you allocate cognitive resources to work instead of sensory management. Your productivity increases because you're not constantly distracted and drained by sensory input.

Communication Flexibility

Remote work enables asynchronous communication through email and messaging platforms. You can take time to process questions and formulate responses. You can contribute to discussions through writing, where your processing time doesn't create awkward pauses.

Video calls still require social monitoring, but you can turn off self-view, reducing the distraction of monitoring your own appearance. You can look at notes instead of maintaining eye contact. The cognitive load decreases.

Schedule Control

Remote work often allows flexible schedules. You can work during your peak productivity hours instead of standard 9-to-5. You can take breaks when you need them instead of following expected break times. You can structure your day around your natural rhythm instead of workplace conventions.

Case Study: Zara's Pandemic Revelation

Zara spent ten years struggling in office environments. She changed jobs frequently, each time hoping the new workplace would somehow work better. Each time, she experienced the same pattern: initial success followed by gradual decline as the cumulative stress of masking and sensory overload accumulated.

"I thought I was bad at jobs. I had excellent technical skills but couldn't seem to sustain employment long-term. Something always went wrong. I'd burn out, my performance would drop, and I'd leave or get let go."

When her company shifted to remote work during the pandemic, Zara's experience changed dramatically. "Suddenly I wasn't exhausted constantly. I could work a full day and still have energy in the evening. My productivity increased. I was completing projects faster and with fewer errors."

Zara's manager noticed the improvement. In their virtual one-on-one, he commented on her increased output and energy. Zara took a risk and explained: working from home eliminated sensory challenges that had been draining her cognitive resources. She could focus on actual work instead of managing constant overstimulation.

"I was terrified he would think I was making excuses or being difficult. But he listened. When the company started discussing return-to-office plans, he advocated for permanent remote work options. I was granted permanent remote status, and my career stabilized for the first time."

Entrepreneurship as Strategic Choice

Some autistic women exit traditional employment entirely, creating businesses that let them control their work environment, schedule, and social interactions. This choice can represent escape from unsustainable situations or strategic decision to optimize their work life.

Environmental Control

Running your own business means designing your work environment to suit your needs. You choose your office setup, lighting, equipment, and sensory conditions. You don't need to request accommodations or justify your environmental preferences.

Client Selection and Interaction Management

Self-employment lets you choose clients and projects. You can decline work that requires intensive masking or extensive in-person meetings. You can set boundaries about communication methods and response times. You design business processes that work with your neurology instead of against it.

Income Variability and Lack of Structure

Entrepreneurship also introduces challenges. Income becomes less predictable. You must manage all business aspects, including marketing and client relations that might require intensive social interaction. Structure must be self-imposed rather than externally provided.

For some autistic women, these challenges outweigh the benefits. For others, the control over work conditions makes the trade-offs worthwhile.

Case Study: Simone's Consulting Transition

Simone spent 15 years in corporate human resources roles. She was excellent at the analytical aspects—designing systems, writing policies, analyzing organizational data. She struggled with the social aspects—employee relations, management coaching, networking events.

"I was constantly exhausted. The job required being 'on' socially all day—reading emotions, navigating conflicts, building relationships. I was competent but depleted."

After her autism diagnosis at 42, Simone reassessed her career. She decided to launch an independent HR consulting practice focused on policy development, compensation analysis, and organizational design—the analytical aspects she enjoyed. She structured her practice to minimize the social aspects that drained her.

"I work primarily asynchronously with clients. I conduct research, develop recommendations, and deliver them in written reports and presentations. I'm not managing daily employee relations or navigating office politics. I control my client load, my schedule, and my environment."

Simone's income initially decreased compared to her corporate salary. But her expenses also decreased—no commute costs, no professional wardrobe expenses, no eating lunch out daily. More important, her quality of life improved dramatically.

"I'm not constantly exhausted anymore. I can work intensely for a few hours, take a break, then work more. I schedule clients when I have energy. I decline projects that would require unsustainable masking.

71

I'm succeeding on my terms instead of trying to fit into corporate templates."

The Path Forward

Workplace challenges for autistic women are real, significant, and poorly understood by most employers and colleagues. But understanding these challenges opens possibilities for addressing them. Some solutions involve individual accommodations—flexible schedules, remote work options, adjusted performance metrics. Some involve systemic changes—redesigning offices for better acoustics, training managers about neurodiversity, reconsidering what "professionalism" requires.

Not every workplace will accommodate your needs. Some environments remain fundamentally incompatible with autistic sensory processing and social interaction patterns. But as awareness grows and remote work becomes more normalized, options expand. You're not failing at work—you're succeeding at something extraordinarily difficult while workplaces slowly adapt to recognize neurological diversity.

What Comes Next

Understanding workplace challenges represents one piece of a larger picture. The next chapter addresses what happens when these challenges accumulate beyond your coping capacity—autistic burnout. The workplace difficulties described here don't just create daily stress. They accumulate into patterns that can lead to complete breakdown of functioning. Recognizing burnout patterns before they reach crisis points becomes crucial for long-term career sustainability.

Key Takeaways

Sensory Environment Impact

- Open office plans create constant sensory overload for many autistic women

- Fluorescent lighting, background noise, and visual distractions fragment concentration
- Sensory management depletes cognitive resources that should be available for work tasks
- Environmental accommodations often cost little but produce significant performance improvements

Social Navigation Challenges

- Unwritten workplace rules govern advancement as much as official policies
- Direct communication styles get penalized despite being efficient and clear
- Office politics require reading subtle social cues that don't come naturally
- Learning explicit rules for workplace diplomacy helps but requires ongoing conscious effort

Communication and Meeting Burden

- Processing delays make real-time verbal participation difficult
- Meeting-intensive cultures exhaust autistic workers disproportionately
- Asynchronous communication often produces better results with less energy expenditure
- Virtual meetings create different challenges but some advantages over in-person formats

Energy Accounting

- Masking extracts significant energy on top of actual work requirements

- Social interactions that energize neurotypical workers deplete autistic workers

- The exhaustion is neurological, not psychological, and requires actual rest not just mindset shifts

- Performance reviews often miss actual contributions while penalizing social performance differences

Work Environment Options

- Remote work provides sensory control and communication flexibility

- Entrepreneurship offers maximum control but introduces different challenges

- Not all workplaces will accommodate neurodivergent needs

- Strategic career choices can reduce masking requirements and increase sustainability

Chapter 5: Understanding Autistic Burnout

The exhaustion accumulates so gradually you might not notice at first. You start needing an extra hour of recovery time after work. Then two hours. Then your entire evening. Weekend recovery extends into Monday morning. Small tasks feel overwhelming. You forget things you've never forgotten before. Skills you've had your entire adult life begin to falter. You're not just tired—something fundamental has broken.

This isn't ordinary burnout, the kind that responds to vacation or stress management. This is autistic burnout, a specific phenomenon that affects many autistic adults, particularly women who have been masking extensively. Understanding autistic burnout means recognizing it as distinct from other forms of exhaustion, identifying warning signs before complete breakdown, and developing recovery strategies that address the actual problem rather than symptoms alone.

What Autistic Burnout Actually Is

Autistic burnout represents a state of pervasive physical, mental, and emotional exhaustion that persists for months or years. It's characterized by chronic tiredness, loss of previously mastered skills, increased sensitivity to sensory input, and reduced capacity for managing basic life tasks. Unlike occupational burnout, which responds to time off work, autistic burnout reflects accumulated strain from existing as an autistic person in environments designed for neurotypical functioning.

The Defining Characteristics

Research identifies three primary features of autistic burnout: chronic exhaustion that doesn't improve with rest, loss of skills you previously managed effectively, and heightened sensitivity to sensory and social input. These features distinguish autistic burnout from depression, anxiety, or occupational burnout, though they can coexist with these conditions.

The exhaustion goes beyond ordinary tiredness. You might sleep 12 hours and wake up feeling like you haven't slept at all. Rest doesn't restore you because the depletion runs deeper than simple fatigue. Your body and brain are signaling that the current level of demand exceeds your sustainable capacity by a wide margin.

Skill loss appears particularly distressing. You might lose the ability to cook meals you've made for years. Phone calls become impossible. Decision-making paralyzes you. Executive function collapses to the point where basic self-care feels overwhelmingly complex. These aren't skills you never had—they're skills you developed and managed successfully until burnout stripped them away.

How It Differs from Depression

Autistic burnout and depression share some surface features—exhaustion, reduced motivation, difficulty with daily tasks. But they differ in important ways. Depression typically involves pervasive sadness, hopelessness, and loss of pleasure in activities. Autistic burnout might not involve emotional flatness at all. You might still want to do things, still feel positive emotions about certain activities, but simply lack the capacity to execute them.

Treatment approaches also differ. Depression responds to therapy and medication targeting mood regulation. Autistic burnout responds to reducing demands, increasing accommodations, and allowing extended recovery time. Treating burnout as depression often fails because the interventions don't address the underlying cause—neurological exhaustion from chronic environmental mismatch.

The Occupational Burnout Distinction

Occupational burnout results from work stress—excessive demands, lack of control, insufficient reward. It improves with vacation, job changes, or stress management. Autistic burnout can include work-related stress but stems fundamentally from the cumulative strain of existing as autistic in a neurotypical world.

You might experience autistic burnout even with a reasonable workload if that work requires constant masking. You might burn out from supposedly relaxing activities if they involve intensive sensory management or social performance. A two-week vacation provides temporary relief but doesn't address the fundamental mismatch between your neurology and environmental demands.

The Warning Signs Professional Women Ignore

Autistic burnout typically develops gradually. Early warning signs appear months before full breakdown, but many women dismiss these signals or attribute them to other causes. Learning to recognize early burnout indicators allows for intervention before complete collapse.

Increased Recovery Time

The first sign often involves needing more recovery time after activities that previously drained you temporarily. You used to need an evening to recover from social events. Now you need a full weekend. Work used to leave you tired but functional in evenings. Now you go straight to bed when you get home, unable to manage dinner or basic self-care.

This pattern indicates that your baseline capacity has decreased. Tasks that once fit within your energy budget now exceed it. You're spending energy reserves instead of operating within sustainable limits.

Reduced Tolerance for Sensory Input

Sounds, lights, textures, and other sensory stimuli that you previously managed become unbearable. The office environment that was always challenging becomes physically painful. Clothing textures you tolerated before now feel intolerable. You start canceling plans because you can't face the sensory demands.

This increased sensitivity reflects a system under stress. Your brain's capacity for processing and filtering sensory information has decreased. You're operating with less filtering capacity, so more sensory input reaches conscious awareness and requires active management.

Skill Regression

You start making mistakes you've never made before. You forget appointments despite using the same calendar system that worked for years. You burn dinner you've cooked successfully hundreds of times. You can't follow conversations you'd normally understand easily. Previously automatic skills now require conscious effort or fail entirely.

Skill regression frightens many women. They interpret it as cognitive decline or early dementia. In autistic burnout, it reflects temporary capacity loss from exhaustion, not permanent neurological damage. But the experience remains terrifying, particularly if you don't understand what's happening.

Increased Shutdowns or Meltdowns

You experience more frequent shutdowns—periods where you can't speak, process language, or interact with others. Or you experience meltdowns—periods of emotional overwhelm that result in crying, angry outbursts, or other intense emotional expression. These episodes increase in frequency and intensity as burnout progresses.

Each shutdown or meltdown signals that you've exceeded your capacity. The threshold for overwhelm decreases as burnout deepens. Situations you previously managed with effort become impossible. The increased frequency indicates your system is near collapse.

Case Study: Lauren's Three-Year Decline

Lauren worked as a graphic designer. She loved the creative aspects of her job and maintained high performance for seven years. Then subtle changes began appearing.

"I started needing more time to complete projects. Work that previously took me three days was taking five. I attributed this to the projects getting more complex or me being perfectionistic. I didn't recognize it as a warning sign."

Lauren's recovery time increased. She stopped seeing friends on weeknights because she needed that time to decompress. Then weekends filled with recovery needs too. She declined social invitations, canceled plans, and gradually withdrew from activities outside work.

"My partner noticed before I did. He pointed out that I was sleeping more—going to bed at 8 PM, sleeping until 7 AM, napping on weekends. He asked if I was depressed. I said no, I was just tired from work."

Skills began failing. Lauren started missing deadlines despite building in extra time. She forgot client meetings. She made design errors she'd never made before. Her supervisor expressed concern about her recent performance decline. Lauren pushed harder, trying to compensate through longer hours and more effort.

"I thought if I just worked harder, I could overcome whatever was wrong. I didn't understand that working harder was making the problem worse. I was already depleted, and increased effort depleted me further."

After three years of gradual decline, Lauren experienced complete breakdown. She stopped being able to work. She couldn't leave her house. She couldn't make simple decisions like what to eat. Her partner took her to a doctor who initially diagnosed severe depression. Antidepressants didn't help.

"Finally, I saw a psychologist who specialized in autism. She recognized autistic burnout. She explained that I'd been masking extensively at work, that the cumulative strain had exceeded my capacity, and that I'd burned out from chronic overextension. Having a name for what was happening was the first step toward recovery."

Lauren's recovery took 18 months. She didn't return to her previous job. She now works part-time as a freelance designer, controlling her workload and client interactions. She's learning to recognize early warning signs and adjust before reaching crisis again.

Case Study: Tanya's Sudden Collapse

Tanya's burnout appeared sudden to outside observers, though in retrospect, warning signs had been present for months. She worked as an accountant, managing her company's financial reporting. The job required attention to detail, complex analysis, and extensive solo work—all suited to her strengths.

"I thought I was doing fine. I was meeting all my deadlines. My work was accurate. My performance reviews were positive. I didn't realize how much effort I was expending to maintain that performance."

Tanya was masking extensively—suppressing stims, forcing social interactions, managing sensory distress silently. She worked through lunch to avoid the noisy break room. She arrived early and left late to minimize contact with colleagues. She appeared professional and competent while silently struggling every day.

"During quarterly close, I worked 60-hour weeks. I told myself it was temporary, just a busy period. But I never fully recovered before the next busy period hit. Each quarter left me more depleted than the last."

The collapse came during tax season. Tanya was working on a complex tax filing when she suddenly couldn't understand the numbers on her screen. "I looked at figures I'd worked with for years and they made no sense. I couldn't remember basic procedures. I felt like my brain had stopped working."

Tanya went home sick. She intended to return after a day or two. Instead, she couldn't get out of bed for a week. She couldn't speak on the phone. She couldn't respond to emails. Basic self-care became overwhelming. Her partner called her doctor, concerned about severe depression.

"The doctor did depression screening and found only mild symptoms. She asked about autism, and I said I'd never been evaluated. She referred me to a specialist who diagnosed both autism and autistic burnout."

Tanya took medical leave for three months. She spent the first month doing almost nothing—sleeping, resting, avoiding sensory input. Recovery was slow. After returning to work part-time, she worked with her employer to implement accommodations: a private office, flexible hours, reduced meeting attendance, and permission to work from home during high-stress periods.

"I'm still recovering two years later. I manage my energy carefully now. I recognize that I have limits and that pushing past them doesn't prove strength—it creates burnout."

Skill Loss, Chronic Exhaustion, and Shutdowns

The three primary features of autistic burnout—skill loss, exhaustion, and increased shutdown frequency—interact and reinforce each other. Understanding how these features manifest helps recognize burnout in yourself or others.

Skill Loss Patterns

Skills fail in predictable patterns during burnout. Executive function skills typically fail first—planning, organizing, time management, decision-making. You might maintain technical skills while losing the ability to manage the logistical aspects of using those skills.

Social and communication skills often fail next. You might lose the ability to make phone calls, respond to emails, or engage in small talk. These skills require significant cognitive effort for many autistic people. Under burnout conditions, you lack the resources to sustain that effort.

Self-care skills fail in severe burnout. Cooking becomes too complex. Showering requires too much executive function and sensory tolerance. Even choosing what to wear can exceed your decision-making capacity. These skill losses frighten many people because they affect basic independent living.

The good news: skill loss in autistic burnout is typically temporary. With adequate rest and reduced demands, skills gradually return. The process takes time—often months—but recovery is possible when the underlying burnout gets addressed.

The Exhaustion That Rest Doesn't Fix

The exhaustion of autistic burnout persists despite sleep. You might sleep 10-12 hours and wake up feeling as tired as when you went to bed. This happens because the exhaustion isn't sleep debt—it's neurological depletion from chronic overextension.

Imagine your nervous system as a battery. Normal daily activities discharge the battery somewhat. Sleep recharges it. But autistic burnout represents a battery that's been overdrawn for so long that it's damaged its capacity to hold a charge. Sleep allows some recovery, but the capacity has decreased. Full recharge requires extended periods of minimal discharge—meaning minimal demands, extensive rest, and supported recovery.

This exhaustion affects everything. You might have energy for one small task per day. Grocery shopping exhausts you for two days. A single phone call drains your capacity for hours. The exhaustion goes beyond physical tiredness to include cognitive and emotional depletion.

Shutdown Frequency and Duration

Shutdowns represent a protective response to overwhelming input or demands. Your brain essentially forces you offline to prevent further damage from overextension. During shutdown, you might lose speech, be unable to process language, struggle to move, or experience significant cognitive slowing.

In autistic burnout, shutdowns occur more frequently and last longer. You might enter shutdown from situations that previously wouldn't trigger this response. Recovery from shutdown takes longer. You might need hours or days to regain full function after shutdown, compared to minutes or hours before burnout.

Increased shutdown frequency signals that your threshold for managing demands has decreased. You're operating closer to your capacity limits constantly, so less additional demand pushes you into shutdown.

Case Study: Alicia's Executive Function Collapse

Alicia worked as a project manager, a role requiring extensive executive function skills. She coordinated timelines, managed resources, tracked multiple projects simultaneously, and communicated with numerous stakeholders. Her systems and organizational skills were excellent—until they weren't.

"I noticed small things first. Forgetting to follow up on emails. Missing details in meeting notes. Needing to check my calendar more frequently. I thought I was just getting busier and needed better systems."

Alicia created more elaborate organizational tools. More detailed checklists. More frequent calendar checks. More reminders. These compensations worked temporarily, but the underlying problem worsened.

"Then I started missing deadlines entirely. I would forget about meetings until I got a call asking where I was. I'd agree to deliverables and then not remember agreeing. My systems weren't failing—my capacity to use systems was failing."

The breakdown came during a major project launch. Alicia was responsible for coordinating multiple teams. On the day of a critical deadline, she couldn't remember what needed to be done. She looked at her carefully maintained project plan and couldn't understand it. The information was there, but she couldn't process it into action.

"I just sat at my desk staring at my computer. My manager came by to check on progress, and I couldn't explain what was wrong. I couldn't form coherent sentences. I was having a shutdown at work, something I'd always managed to avoid before."

Alicia took short-term disability leave. During evaluation, she was diagnosed with autism and autistic burnout. The diagnosis explained the executive function collapse. She'd been compensating for executive function challenges through extensive systems, but burnout depleted the capacity to maintain those systems.

Recovery involved extended rest followed by gradual return to reduced responsibilities. Alicia now works as an individual contributor rather than a manager, focusing on tasks that don't require coordinating multiple stakeholders. Her executive function has recovered partially but hasn't returned to previous levels.

"I'm learning to work within my actual capacity instead of pushing beyond it through compensatory systems. The systems helped for years, but they couldn't indefinitely compensate for the mismatch between my neurology and the demands of project management."

The Burnout-Recovery Cycle

Many autistic women experience recurring patterns of burnout and recovery. They push until burnout forces them to stop. They recover partially. They return to similar demands and burn out again. Breaking this cycle requires understanding the pattern and implementing sustainable changes.

The Push Phase

During the push phase, you're functioning but exceeding sustainable capacity. You might be masking extensively, managing high demands, or operating in challenging environments. The effort feels manageable in the short term. You tell yourself you can sustain this pace, that it's temporary, that things will calm down soon.

Warning signs appear during this phase—increased recovery time, reduced tolerance for sensory input, more frequent shutdowns. But you dismiss these signs or attribute them to temporary circumstances. You push through, drawing on reserves that should be saved for emergencies.

The Crash

Eventually, capacity runs out completely. You hit a wall where you suddenly can't function at the level you've been maintaining. This crash might appear sudden to others, but it represents the culmination of gradual depletion.

During the crash, skills fail, exhaustion becomes overwhelming, and you can't maintain your usual responsibilities. You might take medical leave, quit your job, or dramatically reduce your activities. The crash forces the rest you've been denying yourself.

The Recovery Phase

Recovery requires extended time with reduced demands. You rest extensively. You avoid sensory overload. You engage in activities that restore rather than deplete you. Slowly, capacity returns. Skills come back. Energy improves.

But recovery is slow—typically measured in months, not weeks. And recovery might not return you to your pre-burnout capacity. You might have less resilience, requiring more accommodation and support than before.

The Return and Repeat

After recovering partially, you return to activities. If you return to similar demands without implementing changes, the cycle repeats. Each cycle potentially damages capacity further. Breaking the cycle requires permanent changes to reduce baseline demands.

Case Study: Keiko's Recurring Pattern

Keiko experienced three major burnout episodes over 12 years before recognizing the pattern. Each burnout followed similar trajectories, but she didn't connect them until after her autism diagnosis.

"The first burnout happened in graduate school. I pushed through my dissertation while teaching and thought I just needed to finish the degree. Then I'd have time to recover. I crashed after defending, spent a summer barely functional, and recovered enough to start my first faculty position."

At the faculty position, Keiko excelled initially. Her research productivity was high. Her teaching evaluations were positive. She received grants and published papers. But she was also masking extensively, managing sensory challenges in classroom and lab environments, and pushing beyond sustainable capacity.

"The second burnout came during my tenure review. I'd been pushing hard for five years, accumulating research, teaching, and service. I thought I just needed to make it through tenure. Then I could slow down."

After receiving tenure, Keiko crashed again. She took a semester's leave, recovering partially. She returned to work with good intentions about better work-life balance. But the demands of a tenured position—increased service expectations, graduate student supervision, administrative responsibilities—prevented sustainable pacing.

"The third burnout happened three years after tenure. This time, I ended up hospitalized for severe depression and suicidal thoughts. That's when I finally got an autism evaluation. The psychologist explained that I'd been burning out repeatedly because I kept returning to unsustainable demands."

Understanding the pattern changed Keiko's approach. She worked with her department to restructure her position: reduced teaching load, limited administrative service, focus on research and mentorship. She implemented strict boundaries about work hours and recovery time. She prioritized sustainability over productivity metrics.

"I'm not as 'productive' by traditional measures. But I'm functioning sustainably. I haven't had another major burnout in four years. Breaking the cycle required accepting that I couldn't maintain the pace I'd been attempting."

Why Vacation Doesn't Fix Autistic Burnout

When autistic burnout becomes visible to others, well-meaning people often suggest vacation as a solution. "You just need a break." "Go on vacation and you'll feel better." "You're working too hard." But vacation, while potentially helpful, doesn't fix autistic burnout for several reasons.

The Source Problem

Vacation addresses work-related stress. Autistic burnout stems from chronic environmental mismatch and masking demands that extend beyond work. A vacation removes work stress temporarily but doesn't address the fundamental problem: you're existing as an autistic person in a world designed for neurotypical functioning.

You might experience burnout even with a reasonable work schedule if your entire life requires intensive masking and sensory management. Your daily existence exhausts you in ways vacation can't address.

The Recovery Timeline

Occupational burnout might improve after a week or two of vacation. Autistic burnout requires months or years of reduced demands for full recovery. A two-week vacation provides temporary relief—you might feel somewhat better upon returning—but it doesn't provide the extended recovery period needed for meaningful restoration.

The Return Factor

Even if vacation provides significant relief, returning to the same demands that caused burnout typically recreates the problem. You might feel refreshed after vacation, but if you return to constant masking, sensory overload, and excessive social demands, exhaustion returns quickly.

Sustainable recovery requires changing the baseline conditions, not just taking breaks from them. Vacation provides valuable respite but doesn't constitute a long-term solution without accompanying structural changes.

Mental Health Complications

Autistic burnout frequently coexists with or triggers other mental health conditions. Depression, anxiety, and suicidal ideation appear commonly in autistic women experiencing burnout. These conditions require attention, but treating them without addressing underlying burnout often produces limited results.

Depression and Burnout Intersection

Depression commonly develops during or after burnout. The constant exhaustion, loss of skills, and inability to engage in valued activities create conditions for depression. You might experience hopelessness about recovery, sadness about lost capabilities, and difficulty seeing a path forward.

Treating depression during burnout requires addressing both conditions. Antidepressants might help with mood symptoms but won't resolve the underlying exhaustion and skill loss. Therapy can provide emotional support but needs to account for burnout-specific challenges like reduced cognitive capacity and communication difficulties.

Anxiety as Burnout Signal

Anxiety often intensifies during burnout. You're operating at capacity limits constantly, making everything feel precarious and threatening.

Small demands trigger anxiety because you lack the resources to manage unexpected challenges.

You might develop anticipatory anxiety about tasks you previously managed easily. Phone calls, social events, or work meetings trigger intense anxiety because you know your capacity for managing these situations has decreased. The anxiety isn't irrational—it accurately reflects your reduced capacity.

Suicidality and Crisis

Research indicates elevated suicidality rates among autistic adults, particularly women. Burnout increases suicide risk significantly. The combination of severe exhaustion, skill loss, and reduced quality of life creates feelings of hopelessness. You might think you can't sustain this level of difficulty long-term and see no path to improvement.

Suicidal thoughts during burnout represent a medical emergency requiring immediate professional support. But long-term suicide prevention requires addressing burnout, not just managing crisis symptoms. Recovery from burnout typically reduces suicidal ideation as functioning improves and hope returns.

Case Study: Meredith's Mental Health Crisis

Meredith worked in nonprofit management. She was passionate about her organization's mission and dedicated herself fully to the work. But the job required constant social interaction, frequent travel, and high-stress crisis management. After five years, she crashed.

"I started having panic attacks. Not just anxiety—full panic attacks where I couldn't breathe and thought I was dying. I'd never had panic attacks before. I thought something was medically wrong with me."

Medical evaluation found no physical cause. Meredith's doctor prescribed anti-anxiety medication and recommended therapy. The medication reduced panic attack frequency but didn't address the underlying exhaustion. Therapy focused on anxiety management techniques.

"The therapy helped somewhat with managing anxiety symptoms. But it didn't address why I was so anxious constantly. The therapist suggested I was stressed from work and needed better work-life balance. But I'd already cut back on everything outside work. I had no life to balance."

Meredith's functioning continued declining despite treatment. She started having suicidal thoughts—not from depression but from exhaustion and hopelessness about sustaining such difficulty indefinitely. A crisis line counselor connected her with a clinician specializing in autism, leading to evaluation and diagnosis.

"The diagnosis reframed everything. My anxiety wasn't a primary mental health condition—it was a response to autistic burnout. The panic attacks were happening because I was so depleted that any demand triggered complete overwhelm. Treating the anxiety without addressing the burnout was like treating symptoms while ignoring the disease."

Meredith left her nonprofit position. She took six months away from work entirely, focusing on rest and recovery. She worked with an autism-informed therapist on processing the trauma of unrecognized autism and developing sustainable strategies. Her anxiety decreased dramatically as her burnout resolved.

"I still experience anxiety, but it's manageable now. The panic attacks stopped once I addressed the burnout. The suicidal thoughts resolved once I had hope that life could be sustainable. Diagnosis and burnout recovery literally saved my life."

Creating a Burnout Prevention Plan

Recovering from burnout once it occurs is challenging and time-consuming. Preventing burnout proves far more effective than treating it. Creating a prevention plan requires understanding your specific triggers, warning signs, and recovery needs.

Identifying Your Burnout Triggers

Burnout triggers vary individually. Common triggers include: excessive masking demands, sensory overload, insufficient recovery time, major life changes, loss of coping structures, and social demands that exceed capacity. Identify which specific situations or demands drain you disproportionately.

Keep a log for several weeks, noting your energy levels, activities, and recovery needs. Patterns emerge showing which activities deplete you severely versus those you manage more sustainably. This information guides decisions about what to prioritize, reduce, or eliminate.

Recognizing Your Early Warning Signs

Early warning signs appear before full burnout develops. Learn to recognize your personal warning signs: increased recovery time needs, heightened sensory sensitivity, reduced tolerance for social interaction, minor skill slippages, increased shutdown frequency, difficulty with tasks you usually manage.

When warning signs appear, take immediate action to reduce demands before crisis develops. This might mean canceling plans, requesting accommodations, reducing work hours temporarily, or increasing rest time. Early intervention prevents progression to severe burnout.

Building in Regular Recovery Time

Recovery time isn't optional—it's necessary for sustainable functioning. Schedule regular recovery periods: daily alone time, weekly rest days, monthly reduced-demand periods. Treat recovery time as non-negotiable rather than something you'll do "if you have time."

Recovery time means truly low-demand activities. Rest quietly. Engage in special interests without pressure. Avoid sensory overload. Minimize social interaction. Allow your nervous system to restore resources instead of constantly drawing them down.

Creating Sustainable Structures

Sustainable structures prevent burnout by keeping demands within capacity. This might include: reduced work hours, remote work arrangements, flexible schedules, regular accommodations, environmental controls, and boundaries around social obligations.

These structures shouldn't be emergency measures you implement when crisis threatens. They should be permanent features of your life that prevent demands from exceeding capacity in the first place.

Medical Leave and Recovery Strategies

Sometimes burnout progresses beyond the point where part-time adjustments suffice. Medical leave becomes necessary for recovery. Understanding how to access and use medical leave effectively supports recovery.

Accessing Medical Leave

In the United States, the Family and Medical Leave Act (FMLA) provides up to 12 weeks of unpaid leave for serious health conditions, including mental health crises and burnout-related conditions. Your healthcare provider needs to document that your condition requires leave for treatment or recovery.

Short-term disability insurance, if you have it, might provide income during leave. Some employers offer paid medical leave as part of benefits packages. Check your specific benefits and understand the application process before needing emergency leave.

Using Leave Effectively

Medical leave for burnout recovery requires resisting the urge to stay busy. Early recovery stages need extensive rest—sleeping more, reducing sensory input, minimizing demands. This might feel unproductive, but rest is the intervention that allows recovery.

Mid-recovery stages involve gradually reintroducing activities while monitoring capacity carefully. Don't rush this process. Returning to full demands too quickly creates relapse. Progress appears slow, but sustainable recovery takes time.

Preparing for Return

Returning to work after burnout requires implementing accommodations and structural changes. Don't return to the same conditions that caused burnout. Work with your employer to establish reduced hours, modified duties, environmental accommodations, or work-from-home arrangements.

If your employer won't accommodate your needs, consider whether returning to that job serves your long-term wellbeing. Sometimes recovering from burnout reveals that a particular job or work environment isn't sustainable for you, necessitating career changes.

Case Study: Olivia's Extended Recovery

Olivia experienced severe burnout after ten years working as a therapist. She loved her work but the constant emotional labor and social interaction exhausted her beyond her capacity to recover.

"I took FMLA leave thinking I'd be back in 12 weeks. I used the time to rest, worked with my own therapist on processing the burnout, and felt somewhat better by the end of leave. But I wasn't recovered—I was just less severely burned out."

Olivia returned to work at reduced hours—20 hours per week instead of 40. She saw fewer clients and built more recovery time into her schedule. This arrangement helped but didn't fully prevent burnout recurrence.

"After six months back, I was declining again. My supervisor suggested I wasn't cut out for clinical work. That devastated me because I loved working with clients. But the structure of traditional therapy practice was unsustainable for me."

Olivia took additional leave through short-term disability. She spent this time researching alternative practice structures. She decided to establish a private practice specializing in neurodivergent clients, using video sessions exclusively and limiting her client load.

"Recovery took almost two years total. The first year involved extensive rest. The second year involved gradually building my practice while maintaining careful boundaries. I now work 15-20 hours per week, see clients via video, and take regular breaks. My income is lower than in traditional practice, but I'm sustainable."

Looking Toward Prevention

Autistic burnout causes immense suffering and can damage capacity for years. But it's also preventable through early recognition, appropriate accommodations, and sustainable pacing. The next chapter addresses one strategy for prevention: unmasking, the process of gradually reducing the constant performance of appearing neurotypical.

Unmasking doesn't solve all workplace challenges or guarantee burnout prevention. But it does reduce one major source of depletion—the constant cognitive effort of appearing neurotypical. Learning when, how, and with whom to unmask safely becomes part of creating sustainable professional life.

What We've Learned

Understanding autistic burnout—what it is, how it develops, how it differs from other conditions, and how to prevent or recover from it—provides essential knowledge for long-term professional sustainability. Burnout isn't personal failure or weakness. It's a predictable response to chronic overextension of capacity.

Recovery is possible but requires time, reduced demands, and often significant life restructuring. Prevention is preferable, requiring ongoing attention to capacity limits, early warning signs, and the balance between demands and recovery. With proper understanding and support, you can develop sustainable patterns that allow professional success without destroying your health in the process.

Key Takeaways

Understanding Burnout

- Autistic burnout is chronic exhaustion, skill loss, and increased sensory sensitivity from sustained environmental mismatch

- It differs from depression and occupational burnout in causes, symptoms, and treatment approaches

- Recovery takes months or years, not weeks, and requires reducing baseline demands

- Warning signs appear before full burnout, allowing intervention if recognized early

Recognizing Patterns

- Increased recovery time, reduced sensory tolerance, and skill regression signal developing burnout

- Shutdowns increase in frequency and duration as burnout progresses

- Many autistic women experience recurring burnout cycles without recognizing the pattern

- Breaking the cycle requires permanent changes to demands and accommodations

Recovery Requirements

- Rest alone doesn't fix autistic burnout; extended periods with reduced demands are necessary

- Vacation provides temporary relief but doesn't constitute adequate recovery

- Medical leave may be necessary for severe burnout; use leave time for actual recovery
- Return to work requires accommodations and structural changes to prevent recurrence

Mental Health Connections

- Depression, anxiety, and suicidal ideation commonly accompany autistic burnout
- These conditions require treatment but addressing burnout is essential for sustained improvement
- Treating mental health symptoms without addressing underlying burnout produces limited results
- Suicidality during burnout represents medical emergency requiring immediate professional support

Prevention Strategies

- Identify personal burnout triggers through careful observation of energy patterns
- Learn your specific early warning signs and respond immediately when they appear
- Build regular recovery time into routine rather than waiting for crisis
- Create sustainable structures that keep demands within capacity long-term

Chapter 6: The Unmasking Revolution

You've spent decades learning to appear neurotypical. You studied social rules like textbooks. You practiced facial expressions in mirrors. You suppressed stims, forced eye contact, and translated constantly between your natural processing and expected behaviors. The masking became so automatic you might not consciously recognize doing it anymore. But the cost persists—exhaustion, disconnection from yourself, and the persistent feeling that no one knows the real you.

Unmasking represents a revolutionary act for autistic women who have built their professional identities on appearing neurotypical. It means gradually revealing your authentic autistic self, reducing the constant performance, and allowing your natural processing style to show. But unmasking isn't simple. It requires careful consideration of safety, strategic choices about when and how to unmask, and rebuilding trust in yourself after years of suppression.

Why Unmasking Matters for Long-Term Health

The research on masking and autistic women's health shows clear patterns. Higher masking correlates with worse mental health outcomes—increased depression, anxiety, and suicidal ideation. The cognitive effort of constant masking contributes to exhaustion and burnout. Living behind a mask prevents authentic connection and creates identity confusion. Unmasking addresses these problems at their source.

The Identity Recovery Problem

Decades of masking can create confusion about your authentic self. You've spent so long performing a neurotypical character that you might not know your actual preferences, needs, or natural responses. Unmasking provides the space to rediscover yourself—what you genuinely enjoy, how you naturally communicate, what brings you peace versus what you've been told should bring you joy.

Many women describe unmasking as meeting themselves for the first time. They discover preferences they'd suppressed for so long they'd forgotten them. They find natural communication styles that feel more comfortable than their practiced scripts. They reconnect with interests they'd abandoned because they seemed too intense or unusual.

This identity recovery matters beyond personal satisfaction. Knowing yourself authentically allows better decision-making about relationships, careers, and life structures. You can design a life that suits your actual needs instead of trying to force yourself into a template designed for someone else.

The Energy Conservation Benefit

Masking extracts enormous energy. Every hour spent masking depletes cognitive resources that could be used for other purposes. Unmasking reclaims this energy. You're no longer running two programs simultaneously—appearing neurotypical and doing your actual tasks. You can focus your full resources on what matters to you.

The energy savings appear gradually. As you reduce masking, you might notice feeling less exhausted after social interactions. You might have energy in evenings for activities instead of just collapse and recovery. You might sustain your current workload without burnout constantly threatening. The freed cognitive resources allow for richer engagement with life.

The Connection Authenticity

Relationships built on a masked version of yourself remain superficial by necessity. The other person knows your performance, not you. They respond to the character you've created, not your authentic self. These relationships might be pleasant but lack genuine intimacy.

Unmasking allows authentic connection. You reveal your actual thoughts, preferences, and processing style. People respond to the real you. This creates the possibility for genuine intimacy—being known and accepted as yourself rather than as your performance.

Not everyone will accept your authentic self. Some relationships might end as you unmask. But the relationships that survive gain depth and authenticity. You're known rather than merely seen.

The Fear of Being Found Out

Many autistic women who have masked successfully for decades carry intense fear about being "found out." They've built careers, relationships, and identities on appearing neurotypical. Unmasking threatens these structures. What if people reject you? What if your career suffers? What if you lose everything you've built?

These fears are legitimate. Autism stigma persists. Not everyone responds positively to learning someone is autistic. Some professional environments punish neurodivergence despite claiming to value diversity. The fear reflects realistic assessment of potential risks.

The Cost-Benefit Calculation

Deciding to unmask requires weighing potential costs against current suffering. Continuing to mask preserves your current situation but maintains exhaustion, disconnection, and risk of burnout. Unmasking introduces social and professional risks but offers relief from constant performance.

Neither option is risk-free. The question becomes: which risks are you willing to take? The risks of continued masking or the risks of gradual unmasking?

For many women, the tipping point comes when masking becomes unsustainable. You can't maintain the performance anymore. Burnout forces the issue. At that point, controlled unmasking becomes preferable to collapse and involuntary revelation of struggles.

Worst-Case Scenario Planning

Fear often loses power when examined directly. What's the actual worst-case scenario if you unmask and people respond badly? You might lose some relationships—painful, but survivable. You might need to change jobs—difficult, but possible. You might face discrimination—illegal and addressable through proper channels.

Planning for worst-case scenarios reduces their power. If you know what you'd do if the worst happens, the fear of the unknown decreases. You're not hoping nothing bad happens—you're prepared to handle problems if they arise.

Most unmasking experiences don't result in worst-case scenarios. Many people respond with understanding, support, or simple acceptance. But knowing you can survive bad outcomes makes the risk manageable.

Case Study: Rita's Gradual Revelation

Rita worked as a librarian for 15 years before receiving her autism diagnosis at age 42. She'd masked her entire career, appearing socially competent despite constant internal struggle. The diagnosis created a choice: continue masking or begin unmasking.

"I was terrified. I'd built my professional reputation on being reliable, pleasant, and adaptable. I worried that revealing my autism would destroy that reputation. People would see me as less competent or difficult to work with."

Rita decided to unmask gradually, starting in the safest context she could identify—her close friend group. She explained her diagnosis and what it meant for how she processed the world. Her friends responded with support and curiosity. This positive initial experience gave Rita confidence to continue.

"Next, I told my supervisor. I explained that I'd been diagnosed and requested some simple accommodations—permission to wear headphones while working, flexibility to decline certain social events, and written communication for complex instructions. My supervisor was supportive. He said he'd noticed I seemed more comfortable working independently and appreciated understanding why."

Rita began unmasking incrementally at work. She stopped forcing eye contact during every conversation. She stimmed subtly—tapping her fingers, shifting her weight. She declined some social invitations without elaborate excuses. These small changes felt enormous initially but became easier with practice.

"After six months, I realized I was significantly less exhausted. I could work a full day and still have energy in the evening. I stopped needing entire weekends to recover. The difference was dramatic."

Rita's professional relationships didn't suffer from unmasking. Most colleagues didn't notice the changes. Those who did typically responded neutrally or positively. Rita's work quality remained high—arguably improved because she was using more of her cognitive resources for actual work instead of masking.

"I wish I'd understood this earlier. I spent 15 years exhausting myself unnecessarily. But I also understand why I masked—I needed to protect myself in environments that might not have been safe for an openly autistic person. Unmasking required having the power and security to take that risk."

Case Study: Leah's Coming Out Process

Leah worked in tech sales, a field requiring extensive social performance. After her autism diagnosis at 35, she decided to be openly autistic at work, reasoning that hiding required too much energy and prevented authentic connection.

"I announced it in a team meeting. I said I'd recently been diagnosed autistic and wanted to share this with my colleagues. I explained briefly what that meant for me—that I communicated more directly than neurotypical norms, that I needed certain accommodations, and that I might process information differently."

The team response was mixed. Most colleagues reacted with support or neutral acceptance. One colleague expressed skepticism, suggesting Leah didn't "seem" autistic. Another made jokes about autism stereotypes, though he stopped after Leah addressed it directly.

"The hardest part was people suddenly treating me differently. Some colleagues became overly helpful, offering assistance I didn't need. Others became awkward, seeming unsure how to interact with me. I had to explicitly tell people I was the same person I'd been before the announcement—just now you knew why I did certain things."

Over several months, relationships normalized. Colleagues adjusted to Leah's direct communication style. She stopped forcing herself to laugh at jokes she didn't understand. She declined social events without guilt. She requested accommodations—working from home during high-stress periods, receiving advance notice for meeting topics, having written agendas.

"My sales numbers actually improved after I stopped using so much energy on masking. I could focus on building genuine client relationships instead of performing neurotypical social behaviors. Clients responded well to my straightforward communication style."

Leah's experience highlights both the benefits and challenges of rapid unmasking. The immediate relief from reduced masking came with a period of social awkwardness as relationships adjusted. But for Leah, the trade-off was worthwhile.

"I can't imagine going back to constant masking. Yes, some relationships became more complicated. But I'm living authentically, and the exhaustion that dominated my life for years has decreased dramatically."

Gradual Unmasking Process

Most autistic women benefit from gradual unmasking rather than sudden revelation. Gradual unmasking allows you to test responses, build confidence, and adjust your approach based on feedback. It provides control over the process instead of forcing sudden change.

Identifying Safe Starting Points

Begin unmasking in the safest contexts available. This might be with close friends who you trust to respond supportively. It might be in online communities of other autistic people where you can practice authentic expression without professional risk. It might be at home with family members who love you unconditionally.

Safe starting points share characteristics: relationships with established trust, contexts where mistakes don't carry severe consequences, people who have demonstrated acceptance of difference. Starting in these contexts builds confidence before attempting unmasking in higher-stakes situations.

Incremental Changes

Unmasking incrementally means making small changes rather than dramatic shifts. You might stop forcing eye contact with one trusted colleague before extending this to others. You might stim subtly in private before stimming more visibly in public. You might use direct communication in written form before attempting it verbally.

Each small change provides data. How do people respond? How does it feel? What's the cost-benefit ratio? This information guides your next steps. Changes that go well encourage further unmasking. Changes that produce negative responses suggest areas requiring more caution.

Building Skills While Unmasking

Unmasking doesn't mean abandoning all social skills—it means distinguishing between authentic accommodation to social contexts and exhausting masking. You can maintain professional communication standards while being more authentic. You can adjust your communication style for different audiences without hiding your autistic traits.

The difference: accommodation involves conscious, chosen adjustment that remains sustainable. Masking involves constant suppression of your natural style to meet neurotypical norms, exhausting you in the process. Learning to accommodate without masking requires practice and self-awareness.

Case Study: Angela's Selective Unmasking

Angela worked as a professor, teaching large lectures and conducting research. After her autism diagnosis at 48, she chose to unmask selectively rather than universally.

"I decided to be openly autistic in some contexts but continue masking in others. This wasn't about shame—it was strategic risk management. Some environments felt safe for unmasking. Others didn't."

In her research lab, Angela unmasked significantly. She explained her autism to lab members, implemented autism-friendly practices (clear communication, structured meetings, sensory accommodations), and allowed her natural processing style to show. Lab productivity increased because Angela was using more energy for actual research and mentorship.

In faculty meetings, Angela continued masking to some degree. "Faculty meetings involved politics and power dynamics where neurodivergence might be used against me. I didn't trust that environment enough to fully unmask. I maintained professional performance while saving energy by limiting meeting attendance and contributions."

In lectures, Angela found a middle ground. "I explained to students that I was autistic and what that meant for my teaching style. I told them I might not always make eye contact, that I preferred written questions to verbal ones, and that my communication style was direct.

Most students appreciated the clarity. It also helped neurodiverse students feel more comfortable."

Angela's selective approach allowed her to reduce masking's toll while managing professional risks. She unmasked where it was safe and beneficial, maintained necessary professional performance where it wasn't, and carefully navigated the gray areas.

"Perfect authenticity isn't always possible or even desirable. I'm authentic where I can be, strategic where I must be, and learning to distinguish between the two. That's good enough."

Who Deserves to See the Real You

Unmasking raises questions about authenticity and privacy. Do you owe anyone your unmasked self? Should you unmask with everyone or selectively? These questions lack universal answers—your decisions depend on your values, circumstances, and needs.

The Inner Circle Principle

Many autistic women apply an inner circle principle: closer relationships receive more unmasked authenticity, while distant relationships receive more masking. Your partner, close friends, and family might see you largely unmasked. Professional colleagues might see partial unmasking. Casual acquaintances might see mostly masked presentation.

This graduated approach makes sense practically. Intimacy requires authenticity. Casual interactions don't. You're not being dishonest with acquaintances by masking—you're making reasonable decisions about privacy and energy expenditure.

The principle requires defining your circles and deciding what each circle receives. Close friends might see stims, meltdowns, and unfiltered communication. Work colleagues might see direct communication and accommodations but not the full extent of your struggles. Service workers might see basic professional courtesy with minimal unmasking.

Safety as Primary Consideration

Safety should guide unmasking decisions. You don't owe authenticity to people who might use that information to harm you. If unmasking with certain people creates professional or personal risk, maintaining masking in those contexts protects you.

This isn't paranoia—it's realistic assessment. Not everyone responds positively to autism. Some people hold prejudiced views. Some environments punish neurodivergence despite official diversity policies. Protecting yourself through strategic masking represents rational risk management.

As you gain more power—career stability, financial security, supportive relationships—the risks of unmasking decrease. Early career professionals often need to mask more than established experts. Financial dependence requires more masking than independence. Building power increases your capacity for authentic self-expression.

Reciprocity and Mutuality

Some relationships deserve unmasked authenticity because they offer reciprocal vulnerability and acceptance. People who share their authentic selves with you, who accept your neurodivergence, who support your needs—these people earn access to your unmasked self.

Relationships lacking reciprocity don't require full authenticity. If someone expects you to accommodate their needs but won't accommodate yours, limiting your unmasking with them maintains appropriate boundaries. Authenticity should flow in healthy relationships, not be demanded from only one party.

Strategic Masking vs. Authentic Living

Unmasking doesn't require abandoning all social accommodation or presenting the same way in every context. Strategic masking— conscious, limited performance for specific purposes—differs from chronic masking that exhausts you constantly.

The Consciousness Factor

Strategic masking involves conscious choice. You decide when, where, and how much to mask based on cost-benefit analysis. Chronic masking operates automatically, suppressing your natural responses constantly without conscious choice. The difference between them is control.

Conscious strategic masking might occur in specific situations: job interviews, formal presentations, interactions with authority figures who might discriminate. You choose to mask temporarily because the situation warrants it. Afterwards, you can unmask again.

Chronic masking operates constantly. You mask automatically in all social situations, potentially even when alone. The distinction has disappeared. You're always performing, always translating, always suppressing. This creates exhaustion and identity loss.

Cost-Benefit Decision-Making

Strategic masking requires evaluating whether the benefits justify the costs for specific situations. A job interview might warrant masking— the stakes are high and the duration limited. A casual social event might not—the stakes are lower and extended masking would exceed the value of attendance.

This calculation considers: duration of masking required, stakes of the situation, availability of recovery time afterward, current capacity level, importance of the goal. Making these calculations explicitly helps distinguish situations warranting masking from those where unmasking serves you better.

Maintaining Flexibility

You don't need consistent rules about masking across all contexts. Flexibility serves you better than rigid principles. You might mask significantly in some professional settings, minimally with close friends, and somewhere in between with extended family. Each context receives your considered response based on safety, goals, and capacity.

This flexibility isn't inconsistency—it's adaptive response to varying circumstances. The goal isn't perfect authenticity everywhere but sustainable functioning that honors your needs while achieving your goals.

Case Study: Monica's Masking Continuum

Monica developed what she calls her "masking continuum" after her autism diagnosis at 40. Instead of binary choices about masking or unmasking, she created a graduated approach.

"I rated contexts on a scale from 1 to 10—1 being fully unmasked and 10 being maximum masking. Then I decided what level of masking each regular situation in my life required."

At home alone: Level 1—complete unmasking. Monica stimmed freely, made whatever sounds felt natural, wore comfortable clothes regardless of appearance, and didn't monitor her facial expressions or communication style.

With her partner: Level 2—minimal masking. Monica explained her needs, unmasked generally but sometimes translated or explained her autistic processing for mutual understanding.

With close friends: Level 3—light masking. Monica was openly autistic but sometimes translated or accommodated neurotypical communication styles for clarity.

At work with colleagues: Level 5—moderate masking. Monica maintained professional communication standards, accommodated neurotypical expectations somewhat, but didn't hide her autism or suppress reasonable accommodations.

In client meetings: Level 7—significant masking. Monica's consulting work required projecting confidence and reading social dynamics carefully. She masked substantially during client interactions but recovered afterward.

At formal networking events: Level 9—nearly maximum masking. Monica attended these events rarely because they required exhausting levels of performance. When attending, she masked extensively and limited duration.

"This system helps me make conscious decisions about energy expenditure. I know that Level 9 masking is unsustainable for more than an hour or two. Level 5 masking is sustainable for a workday if I have recovery time. Level 1-3 is where I can actually rest and recover."

Monica's continuum allows strategic masking without chronic exhaustion. She knows which situations require which levels and makes conscious choices about attendance and participation based on her current capacity.

Rediscovering Your Interests and Preferences

Years of masking often involve suppressing interests, preferences, and aspects of yourself that seemed too autistic. Unmasking includes reclaiming these suppressed parts. This process can feel strange— discovering preferences you'd forgotten you had or revealing interests you'd hidden for decades.

Interest Reclamation

Many autistic women abandon or hide their special interests because they seem too intense or unusual. As an adult, you might not even remember what naturally fascinates you because you've suppressed it for so long.

Unmasking creates space to explore interests without judgment. What captures your attention naturally? What could you research or discuss for hours? What topics make you feel energized rather than drained? Following these curiosities reclaims part of your authentic self.

Your interests might differ from neurotypical norms in intensity or focus. You might care deeply about topics others find boring. You might collect extensive knowledge about subjects others consider trivial. These aren't defects—they're features of your autistic processing that you've been trained to hide.

Preference Discovery

Preferences you've suppressed for years might resurface as you unmask. You might discover you genuinely hate certain textures, tastes, or sensory experiences you've been tolerating. You might realize you prefer solitude to socializing, written to verbal communication, or routine to novelty.

Some of these preferences contradict messages you've received about proper adult behavior. You might prefer comfortable clothes to fashionable ones, quiet evenings alone to social events, or deep focus on interests to varied activities. Allowing yourself to honor these preferences instead of forcing yourself into neurotypical expectations improves wellbeing significantly.

Natural Communication Style

Your natural communication style might differ from what you've been performing. You might be more direct, literal, detailed, or structured than neurotypical communication norms expect. Unmasking allows you to communicate naturally instead of constantly translating.

Some people appreciate directness. Others find it off-putting. You can't control others' reactions, but you can control whether you exhaust yourself translating constantly. Using your natural style with people who appreciate it creates authentic connection. Limiting interaction with people who can't accept your style maintains your energy.

Case Study: Veronica's Interest Renaissance

Veronica spent her childhood fascinated by insects. She collected them, studied them, drew detailed sketches, and read every book about entomology she could find. But by adolescence, she'd learned that girls weren't supposed to be interested in bugs. She suppressed this interest, pretending to care about more socially acceptable topics.

"For 30 years, I barely thought about insects. I'd trained myself not to notice them, not to feel curious about them. I'd buried that interest so deeply I'd almost forgotten it existed."

After her autism diagnosis at 45, Veronica started unmasking. As part of this process, her therapist asked about childhood interests. When Veronica mentioned insects, she felt unexpected emotion.

"I started crying talking about insects. I hadn't realized how much I'd lost by suppressing that interest. It wasn't just about bugs—it was about denying a fundamental part of myself for decades."

Veronica began reengaging with her insect interest. She joined online entomology communities. She visited natural history museums. She started photographing insects in her garden. The interest that had once dominated her childhood returned immediately and intensely.

"My husband was bemused. He'd never seen me this excited about anything. I was reading research papers on insect behavior, watching documentaries, planning vacations around butterfly migrations. I felt alive in a way I hadn't felt since childhood."

Reclaiming her interest improved Veronica's life quality significantly. She had something that energized rather than depleted her. She joined communities of people who shared her fascination. She stopped trying to be interested in topics that bored her to fit in socially.

"I can't believe I denied myself this for 30 years because I thought it was weird for a woman to care about insects. That's society's problem, not mine. I'm done hiding what brings me joy."

Building Self-Trust After Suppression

Years of masking teach you not to trust yourself. You learn that your natural responses are wrong, that your instincts need correction, that your preferences are invalid. Unmasking requires rebuilding trust in your own perceptions and judgments.

Validity of Your Experiences

Your sensory experiences are real and valid even if others don't share them. The fluorescent lights that give you headaches genuinely hurt, regardless of others being unbothered. The noise level that overwhelms you actually exceeds your processing capacity, regardless of others finding it tolerable. Your experiences are data, not overreaction.

Rebuilding self-trust means accepting your experiences as valid information rather than problems to overcome. If something hurts, it hurts. If something exhausts you, it exhausts you. Your body and brain are providing accurate feedback about your experience. Trust that feedback instead of dismissing it.

Permission to Have Needs

You have needs that differ from neurotypical norms. You need more recovery time, more predictability, more sensory control, more direct communication. These needs aren't excessive or difficult—they're just different from neurotypical needs.

Self-trust involves accepting that you can have needs without being burdensome. Requesting accommodations isn't demanding special treatment—it's seeking equivalent access. Declining activities that exceed your capacity isn't weakness—it's appropriate boundary-setting. Your needs deserve respect, including from yourself.

Learning to Say No

Masking often involves people-pleasing—saying yes to requests regardless of capacity, attending events you don't want to attend, suppressing discomfort to avoid bothering others. Self-trust requires learning to say no without excessive justification.

You don't need to provide detailed explanations for declining invitations or requests. "I'm not available" or "That doesn't work for me" constitute complete answers. Rebuilding self-trust involves recognizing that you don't owe others access to your time, energy, or presence at the cost of your wellbeing.

Case Study: Naomi's Boundary Revolution

Naomi spent 40 years saying yes to every request. She attended events she didn't want to attend, helped with projects she didn't have time for, and maintained friendships that exhausted her. She thought saying no made her selfish or difficult.

"After my autism diagnosis, my therapist asked me to track how I spent my time and how each activity affected my energy. The results shocked me. I was spending 70% of my non-work time on activities I didn't enjoy and that depleted me. I did them because I felt obligated."

Naomi started saying no—tentatively at first. She declined a social invitation, expecting backlash or guilt. Her friend said "okay, maybe next time" and that was it. No drama. No guilt trip. The world didn't end.

"I realized I'd been creating problems that didn't exist. I assumed people would be upset if I said no, but most people were fine with it. I was the one making myself miserable by always saying yes."

Naomi gradually expanded her boundary-setting. She stopped attending events that required excessive sensory tolerance. She declined committee work that didn't interest her. She reduced her social calendar to include only genuine friends, not acquaintances she maintained out of obligation.

"Some relationships ended as I stopped doing all the maintenance work. That hurt initially. But I realized those relationships only existed because I was doing 100% of the work. If someone only wants to be in my life when I'm constantly accommodating them, that's not a real friendship."

Learning to say no reclaimed enormous amounts of time and energy. Naomi used this recovered capacity for activities she actually enjoyed and relationships that were genuinely reciprocal. Her quality of life improved dramatically.

"I wish I'd learned this 20 years ago. But I couldn't learn it until I trusted myself enough to believe my needs mattered. Unmasking gave me that self-trust."

The Ongoing Process

Unmasking isn't a destination you reach and complete. It's an ongoing process of balancing authenticity with accommodation, safety with self-expression, and energy conservation with relationship maintenance. The balance shifts as circumstances change.

Accepting Imperfection

You won't always make the right decisions about when to mask or unmask. Sometimes you'll mask more than necessary, exhausting yourself needlessly. Sometimes you'll unmask in situations where more caution would have served you better. This is normal. Learning involves mistakes.

Perfectionism about unmasking defeats the purpose. The goal isn't perfect authenticity in all situations—it's reducing chronic masking enough to decrease exhaustion and increase connection. Imperfect progress still represents progress.

Contextual Adjustment

What works in one life stage might not work in another. Early career requires more masking than established expertise. Financial precarity requires more caution than security. Unsupportive environments require more protection than accepting ones.

As your circumstances change, your unmasking strategy can adjust. You might unmask gradually as you gain security. You might temporarily increase masking during high-stakes periods. Flexibility serves you better than rigid commitment to either full masking or complete unmasking.

Community Connection

Connecting with other autistic people supports the unmasking process. In autistic spaces, you can practice being unmasked without translating. You can share experiences with people who understand them intuitively. You can develop language for aspects of yourself you've struggled to articulate.

These connections provide models for authenticity and reassurance that you're not alone. Seeing other autistic women living authentically demonstrates that it's possible. Learning from others' experiences helps you navigate your own process more effectively.

Moving Forward

Unmasking represents one component of building sustainable professional life as an autistic woman. It reduces energy expenditure on performance, allowing more resources for actual work and wellbeing. It creates possibility for authentic connection. It rebuilds relationship with yourself after years of suppression.

But unmasking alone doesn't solve all workplace challenges. Creating truly sustainable professional life requires multiple strategies: appropriate accommodations, supportive environments, boundary maintenance, and ongoing self-awareness. The subsequent chapters will address these additional elements of thriving professionally while autistic.

Looking Ahead

You've learned about the exhaustion of masking, the process of obtaining diagnosis, the specific ways autism manifests in professional women, the workplace challenges you face, the patterns of burnout that threaten sustainability, and now the possibility of unmasking. These pieces together form a foundation for the next stage: building structures and strategies that allow authentic professional success.

The remaining chapters will address practical workplace accommodations, self-advocacy strategies, and career design that works with rather than against your neurology. You're not alone in this process, and you don't have to figure everything out perfectly before taking steps. Progress happens gradually, imperfectly, and in the direction you choose.

Key Takeaways

Health and Identity Benefits

- Unmasking reduces exhaustion from constant performance and reclaims cognitive resources

- Authentic self-expression supports identity recovery after years of suppression

- Genuine connection requires revealing your real self, not just your performance

- Long-term wellbeing improves when you can function more authentically

Managing Fear and Risk

- Fear of unmasking reflects realistic assessment of autism stigma and potential discrimination

- Strategic risk assessment helps distinguish safe unmasking contexts from risky ones

- Worst-case scenario planning reduces fear's power and enables conscious choice

- Safety should guide unmasking decisions; you don't owe authenticity to everyone

Gradual Process

- Starting with safest contexts and incrementally expanding builds confidence

- Selective unmasking allows different levels of authenticity in different contexts

- Strategic masking differs from chronic masking in consciousness and control

- Flexibility serves better than rigid rules about always masking or never masking

Rediscovering Yourself

- Years of masking suppress interests, preferences, and natural communication styles

- Unmasking creates space to reclaim parts of yourself you'd hidden or forgotten

- Your natural preferences and interests deserve expression even if they differ from neurotypical norms

- Self-trust rebuilding involves accepting your experiences and needs as valid

Sustainable Authenticity

- Unmasking is ongoing process, not destination you reach and complete

- Imperfect progress represents real progress; perfectionism defeats the purpose

- Context and circumstances change; unmasking strategies can adjust accordingly

- Connection with autistic community supports unmasking and provides models for authenticity

Chapter 7: Self-Advocacy Without Apology

- You deserve accommodations that allow you to work effectively. This statement might feel radical if you've spent years adapting yourself to impossible environments while blaming yourself for the difficulty. But accommodations aren't special treatment—they're adjustments that provide equal access to employment. The neurotypical person doesn't think twice about the environmental features that support their functioning. You shouldn't either.

- Self-advocacy means requesting what you need without apologizing for needing it. This skill requires understanding your legal rights, making strategic disclosure decisions, communicating effectively about your needs, and responding appropriately to resistance. The process feels daunting initially, but each successful advocacy experience builds confidence and improves your work conditions.

- **Understanding Your Legal Rights**

- In the United States, the Americans with Disabilities Act (ADA) protects qualified individuals with disabilities from employment discrimination. Autism qualifies as a disability under the ADA. This means you have legal protection against discrimination and the right to reasonable accommodations that allow you to perform essential job functions.

- **What the ADA Covers**

- The ADA applies to employers with 15 or more employees. It prohibits discrimination in hiring, firing, promotion, compensation, and all other employment terms and conditions. Employers must provide reasonable accommodations to qualified employees with disabilities unless doing so creates undue hardship.

- Reasonable accommodations are modifications or adjustments to jobs, work environments, or standard employment procedures that enable qualified individuals with disabilities to perform essential job functions. The key word is "reasonable"—accommodations must be effective and feasible for the employer to implement.

- Undue hardship means significant difficulty or expense relative to the employer's size, resources, and business operations. The threshold for undue hardship is high. Most accommodations for autistic employees cost little or nothing to implement. Employers can't deny accommodations simply because they're inconvenient or require minor adjustments to standard procedures.

- **The Interactive Process**

- Once you request accommodation, the ADA requires an interactive process between you and your employer. This collaborative discussion aims to identify your limitations, potential accommodations, and practical solutions. The employer can ask for medical documentation supporting your need for accommodation but can't require disclosure of your specific diagnosis beyond confirming you have a covered disability.

- You initiate the interactive process by requesting accommodation. Your request doesn't need to use specific legal language—simply stating that you need an adjustment due to a medical condition triggers the employer's obligation to engage in the process. From there, you and your employer work together to identify effective accommodations.

119

- **State and Local Protections**

- Many states and localities provide additional protections beyond federal ADA requirements. Some cover smaller employers. Some define disability more broadly. Some provide stronger enforcement mechanisms. Research your specific state and local protections to understand your full rights.

- **Case Study: Melissa's ADA Request Process**

- Melissa worked as a data analyst. After receiving her autism diagnosis at 36, she decided to request accommodations to address sensory challenges and communication preferences that had been draining her for years.

- "I was terrified to disclose. I worried they'd see me as less competent or difficult. But I was also exhausted and heading toward burnout. I needed changes to sustain my job."

- Melissa researched the ADA before approaching her employer. She identified specific accommodations she needed: permission to wear noise-canceling headphones, a desk lamp so she could turn off overhead fluorescent lights, written agendas for meetings, and the option to participate in some meetings via video rather than in person.

- She scheduled a meeting with her supervisor and HR representative. She brought a letter from her doctor confirming she had a condition qualifying as a disability under the ADA and needed accommodations. The letter didn't specify autism—it simply confirmed the disability and need for accommodations.

- "I explained that I had a condition affecting my sensory processing and that certain environmental factors made it difficult for me to concentrate. I presented my accommodation requests and explained how each one would help me work more effectively."

- The company's response was mostly positive. They immediately approved the headphones and desk lamp. They agreed to provide meeting agendas in advance. The video meeting participation required more discussion because the company culture emphasized in-person presence, but HR confirmed it qualified as reasonable accommodation.

- "The whole process took about three weeks from my initial request to full implementation. My work life improved dramatically. I could concentrate better. I wasn't constantly exhausted from sensory overload. My performance actually improved once I had appropriate accommodations."

- Melissa's experience illustrates effective ADA advocacy: researching her rights, identifying specific accommodations, providing medical documentation, and engaging constructively in the interactive process.

- **The Disclosure Decision**

- Requesting formal accommodations under the ADA requires disclosing that you have a disability. This disclosure decision carries both benefits and risks that you must weigh carefully based on your specific circumstances.

- **Benefits of Disclosure**

- Disclosure provides legal protection. Once you've disclosed a disability and requested accommodations, your employer can't discriminate against you based on that disability. You gain access to the interactive process and formal accommodations.

- Disclosure can also improve daily functioning significantly. With appropriate accommodations, you work more effectively, experience less exhaustion, and reduce burnout risk. The relief from having environmental support often outweighs disclosure risks.

- Disclosure sometimes improves relationships with supervisors and colleagues. When people understand that your differences reflect neurological variation rather than personality flaws or lack of effort, they may respond with more understanding and flexibility.

- **Risks of Disclosure**

- Despite legal protections, disclosure carries risks. Some employers discriminate against disabled employees despite the law. Discrimination can be subtle—being passed over for promotions, receiving lower performance ratings, being excluded from opportunities. Proving discrimination is difficult and pursuing legal remedies is stressful and time-consuming.

- Some colleagues respond to disclosure with changed perceptions. They might treat you as less competent, offer unwanted help, or become awkward in interactions. These changed dynamics can be uncomfortable even if not legally discriminatory.

- Disclosure is permanent. Once you've disclosed to an employer, you can't take it back. If you change positions within the company or your supervisor changes, the information remains in your file.

- **Strategic Disclosure Considerations**

- Several factors should guide your disclosure decision. Job security matters—employees with longer tenure and strong performance records face less risk than new employees. Company culture matters—organizations with demonstrated commitment to diversity and inclusion typically respond more positively than those without such commitments.

- Your relationship with your supervisor matters significantly. A supportive supervisor can facilitate accommodations even beyond formal requirements. An unsupportive supervisor might comply minimally while creating obstacles informally.

- Your capacity to sustain current conditions matters. If you're approaching burnout, disclosure risks may be worth taking because continuing without accommodations isn't sustainable.

- **Case Study: Tasha's Selective Disclosure Strategy**

- Tasha received her autism diagnosis while working as a software engineer at a large tech company. She decided on selective disclosure—revealing her autism to HR and her immediate supervisor while not disclosing broadly to colleagues.

- "I wanted formal accommodations and legal protection. But I didn't want my autism to become the defining feature of how all my colleagues saw me. Selective disclosure gave me both protection and some privacy."

- Tasha met with HR to request accommodations: flexible work-from-home options, permission to skip certain social events, and modification of her performance review process to include written self-assessment before verbal discussion. HR documented her disability status and approved the accommodations.

- She then met with her supervisor privately. "I explained that I was autistic and what that meant for my work style. I told him about the formal accommodations HR had approved. I also asked for informal support—clearer project specifications, advance notice of changes, and patience with my direct communication style."

- Her supervisor responded well. "He said he appreciated my directness and that the accommodations made sense. He also said several things about my work style suddenly made sense to him. He'd noticed I preferred written communication and solo work but hadn't understood why."

- Tasha chose not to disclose to her team or colleagues more broadly. "My autism affects how I work, but it's not something I wanted to explain or discuss with everyone. I disclosed to people who needed to know to provide accommodations. That was sufficient."

- This selective approach worked well for Tasha. She received the accommodations and support she needed while maintaining privacy about her diagnosis with most colleagues. Five years later, she's still with the same company and has been promoted twice.

- **Formal vs. Informal Accommodation Requests**

- Accommodations can be obtained formally through the ADA process or informally through direct negotiation with supervisors. Each approach has advantages and disadvantages.

- **Formal Accommodation Process**

- Formal requests trigger legal protections and obligations. You document your disability, specify needed accommodations, and engage in the interactive process. The company documents approved accommodations. This documentation protects you if your supervisor changes, if you move to a different department, or if disputes arise.

- Formal requests also carry downsides. The process involves paperwork and medical documentation. Information goes into your HR file. Multiple people become aware of your disability status. The process can take weeks.

- Formal accommodations make sense when you need significant adjustments, when informal requests have been denied, when you work for a large organization with formal processes, or when you want legal documentation of your accommodations.

- **Informal Accommodation Arrangements**

- Informal accommodations involve direct negotiation with your supervisor without involving HR or the formal ADA process. You explain what you need and why it would help you work more effectively. Your supervisor agrees to provide it.

- Informal arrangements offer advantages: faster implementation, less paperwork, fewer people involved, and more flexibility in modifying arrangements. They work well for minor accommodations, in small organizations, or when you have a good relationship with your supervisor.

- The primary disadvantage: informal accommodations lack legal protection. If your supervisor leaves or changes their mind, you have no documented agreement. If you move to a different department, you must renegotiate. If discrimination occurs, you have less evidence.

- Informal accommodations work well for low-stakes needs in supportive environments. For significant accommodations or when you lack trust in your employer's goodwill, formal requests provide necessary protection.

- **Language That Works**

- How you communicate about your needs significantly affects how people respond. Effective accommodation requests use specific, clear language focused on functional impacts and solutions rather than diagnostic labels or vague problems.

- **Focus on Function, Not Diagnosis**

- Frame accommodation requests around how specific environmental factors affect your work performance. You don't need to explain autism in detail or educate people about neurological differences. Focus on the practical problem and solution.

- Instead of saying: "I'm autistic and struggle with sensory overload in open offices."

- Say: "I have a condition that affects how I process sensory information. The background noise in the open office makes it difficult for me to concentrate on complex analysis. Using noise-canceling headphones would allow me to focus more effectively."

- The second approach provides the same information but frames it practically. You've identified the problem (noise interferes with concentration), explained the impact (difficulty with complex analysis), and proposed a solution (headphones).

- **Be Specific About Accommodations**

- Vague requests like "I need a quieter workspace" give employers too much discretion and may result in inadequate accommodations. Specific requests like "I need permission to wear noise-canceling headphones while working" or "I need to be relocated to a desk away from high-traffic areas" clearly communicate what you need.

- For each accommodation, explain how it helps you perform essential job functions. "Headphones help me concentrate on data analysis" connects the accommodation to job performance. "Video meeting attendance for some meetings would reduce my exhaustion and allow me to participate more effectively" explains the functional benefit.

- **Use "Need" Language Confidently**

- Many autistic women soften accommodation requests excessively: "I was wondering if maybe it might be possible to sometimes work from home?" This tentative language signals that the accommodation is optional rather than necessary.

126

- Instead, use clear need language: "I need to work from home two days per week to manage my condition effectively." This directly states your need without demanding or apologizing.

- You can be direct without being rude. "I need X" differs from "You must give me X." The first states your requirement. The second demands compliance. State your needs clearly and let the interactive process determine how they'll be met.

- **Case Study: Jamila's Accommodation Language Evolution**

- Jamila worked as a technical writer. She struggled with meeting-intensive work culture but didn't know how to request changes without sounding difficult.

- Her first attempt at requesting accommodation failed because of her language choices: "I find meetings kind of draining. Would it be possible for me to maybe skip some of them if I'm busy with other work?"

- Her supervisor responded: "We all find meetings tiring. They're part of the job. You can't skip meetings when you feel like it."

- After receiving coaching on accommodation requests, Jamila tried again, this time with clearer language:

- "I have a condition affecting how I process information. Attending back-to-back meetings prevents me from completing my writing work effectively. I need to limit my meeting attendance to four hours per day and receive advance agendas so I can prepare. I'd like to participate in some meetings asynchronously by reviewing notes and providing written input."

- She provided a doctor's note confirming she had a condition requiring workplace accommodations. This time, her supervisor took the request seriously. HR got involved. They engaged in the interactive process and agreed to meeting limitations and advance agendas.

- "The difference was how I communicated. The first time, I presented it as a preference that was negotiable. The second time, I presented it as a need requiring accommodation. The content was similar, but the framing made all the difference."

- **Common Workplace Accommodations for Autistic Women**

- Accommodations for autistic employees vary based on individual needs, but certain categories appear frequently. Understanding common accommodation types helps you identify what might help you and provides language for requesting similar accommodations.

- **Sensory Accommodations**

- Noise-canceling headphones or earplugs for sound sensitivity. Desk lamps or modified lighting to replace fluorescent lights. Workspace location away from high-traffic areas, loud equipment, or strong scents. Permission to adjust thermostat or use personal heating/cooling devices. Furniture modifications for physical comfort.

- **Communication Accommodations**

- Written agendas provided in advance of meetings. Written follow-up after verbal discussions. Permission to communicate via email rather than phone when possible. Extended time to process questions and formulate responses. Clear, direct feedback rather than implied criticism. Structured one-on-one meetings with supervisors rather than spontaneous check-ins.

- **Schedule and Flexibility Accommodations**

- Flexible work hours to accommodate peak productivity times. Work-from-home options to control environment and reduce social demands. Modified break schedule to allow for necessary recovery time. Advance notice of schedule changes. Reduced or eliminated travel requirements.

- **Meeting and Social Accommodations**

- Limited meeting attendance with clear criteria for required versus optional meetings. Video meeting participation option. Permission to decline social events not directly related to job functions. Structured agenda for meetings rather than open discussions. Written participation options in addition to verbal contributions.

- **Task and Project Accommodations**

- Clear, written project specifications and requirements. Regular, structured feedback rather than waiting for formal reviews. Break large projects into smaller components with interim deadlines. Modified evaluation criteria accounting for different communication styles. Access to quiet space for concentration-intensive tasks.

- **Negotiating Your Specific Needs**

- Effective negotiation involves understanding your needs clearly, communicating them effectively, remaining flexible about implementation methods while firm about underlying requirements, and problem-solving collaboratively when obstacles arise.

- **Identifying Your Core Needs**

- Before requesting accommodations, identify what you actually need versus what you've been doing to cope. You might have been coping by working 60 hours per week when appropriate accommodations would let you work 40. The accommodation you need addresses the underlying problem, not your compensation strategy.

- Ask yourself: What environmental factors create the most difficulty? What aspects of my job drain energy disproportionately? What changes would allow me to work more effectively? What accommodations would prevent burnout?

- Document patterns. Keep a log for several weeks noting which situations drain you most, which environmental factors trigger sensory distress, and which aspects of work you manage sustainably. This data helps identify specific accommodation targets.

- **Finding Win-Win Solutions**

- Frame accommodations as beneficial for both you and your employer. "This accommodation will help me work more effectively" appeals to the employer's interest in your productivity. When possible, propose accommodations that solve problems for the employer while meeting your needs.

- For example, if you need to reduce meeting attendance, frame it as allowing you to spend more time on productive work that benefits the company. If you need flexible hours, explain how it allows you to work during peak productivity times.

- Be open to alternative implementations that meet your underlying need. If you request a private office but the company can't provide one, would a cubicle with higher walls work? If you need to limit meetings, would attending the first half hour of long meetings suffice?

- **Case Study: Kai's Flexible Work Negotiation**

- Kai worked as a consultant. Her job required significant client interaction, extensive travel, and unpredictable schedules—all factors that exhausted her disproportionately. After her autism diagnosis, she decided to request accommodations, but she worried that changing the fundamental nature of her role wouldn't be possible.

- She identified her core needs: reduced travel, more predictable schedule, and control over her environment. She then considered how to meet these needs while still performing her job effectively.

- Kai proposed a restructured role to her supervisor: "I'd like to transition to focusing on remote consulting with reduced travel. I could take on additional clients who prefer video consultations and written reports over in-person meetings. This would allow me to serve more clients overall while working in a way that's more sustainable for me."

- Her supervisor was initially resistant—the company culture valued in-person client relationships. But Kai presented data showing that several clients had requested video options and that remote consulting was becoming more acceptable industry-wide.

- "I framed it as expanding our service offerings and adapting to client preferences, not just accommodating my needs. That reframing made it easier for my supervisor to approve."

- The company agreed to a six-month trial. Kai's client satisfaction remained high. Her productivity increased because she wasn't exhausted from constant travel. After the trial period, the arrangement became permanent and the company started offering remote consulting more broadly.

- "I got my accommodation by finding a way to frame it as beneficial for the company. I couldn't just say 'travel is hard for me.' I had to show how my proposed alternative would work well for the business."

- **Handling Pushback and Discrimination**

- Not all accommodation requests receive supportive responses. Some employers push back against legitimate requests. Some engage in subtle discrimination despite legal obligations.

Knowing how to respond to resistance protects your rights and increases the likelihood of obtaining needed accommodations.

- **Types of Pushback**

- Employers might claim accommodations create undue hardship when they actually don't. They might suggest accommodations aren't necessary for essential job functions. They might propose inadequate alternatives. They might delay the interactive process indefinitely. They might suggest you're not qualified for your position if you need accommodations.

- These responses may reflect ignorance about ADA requirements rather than intentional discrimination. Some employers and supervisors simply don't understand their legal obligations. Education can resolve these situations.

- Other responses reflect resistance to providing accommodations even when legally required. These situations require firmer advocacy and potentially formal complaints.

- **Responding to Pushback Effectively**

- Document everything. Keep copies of all accommodation requests, medical documentation, communications with HR and supervisors, and records of the interactive process. If conversations happen verbally, follow up with written summaries sent via email.

- If your employer claims undue hardship, ask for specific explanation of why the accommodation is too difficult or expensive. Undue hardship has a high legal threshold. Most accommodations for autistic employees don't meet it.

- If your employer suggests the accommodation isn't necessary, provide clear explanation of how the current situation prevents you from performing essential job functions and how the accommodation would resolve this problem.

132

- If your employer proposes inadequate alternatives, explain specifically why the alternative doesn't meet your needs and restate your original request or propose a different effective alternative.

- **When Informal Resolution Fails**

- If your employer refuses to engage in good-faith interactive process or denies reasonable accommodations, you have several options. File a formal complaint with HR if you haven't already. Many companies have internal dispute resolution processes for accommodation disagreements.

- File a charge with the Equal Employment Opportunity Commission (EEOC). The EEOC investigates discrimination claims and can facilitate resolution or provide authorization to file a lawsuit. You must file an EEOC charge before filing a lawsuit.

- Consult with an employment attorney who specializes in disability discrimination. Many offer free initial consultations and work on contingency for discrimination cases. An attorney can assess your situation and advise on the strongest approach.

- **Case Study: Rosa's EEOC Process**

- Rosa worked as a paralegal. After requesting accommodations for her autism—flexible schedule and permission to work from home two days per week—her employer denied the request, claiming all staff needed to maintain regular office hours.

- "They said the accommodations would be unfair to other employees and that flexibility wasn't possible for my position. But other paralegals had flexible arrangements for childcare. The denial seemed discriminatory."

- Rosa documented the denial and filed an internal complaint with HR. HR upheld the denial. She then filed a charge with the EEOC alleging disability discrimination.

- "The EEOC process took several months. An investigator reviewed my complaint, interviewed me and company representatives, and examined documentation. The EEOC found reasonable cause to believe discrimination had occurred."

- Facing an EEOC finding against them, Rosa's employer agreed to mediation. During mediation, they agreed to provide the requested accommodations and paid Rosa for back wages and emotional distress.

- "I didn't want to file a complaint. I wanted them to just provide the accommodations. But sometimes employers don't take accommodation requests seriously until facing legal consequences. The EEOC process worked—I got my accommodations and compensation for the discriminatory denial."

- **Building Allies and Documentation**

- Successful self-advocacy often involves building support networks and maintaining thorough documentation. Both strategies strengthen your position and provide resources when challenges arise.

- **Identifying Potential Allies**

- Workplace allies might include supportive supervisors, HR professionals who understand disability rights, colleagues who've requested accommodations themselves, employee resource groups focused on disability inclusion, or union representatives if you're unionized.

- Look for people who demonstrate understanding of diversity issues, who've advocated for others, or who've shown flexibility in accommodating different work styles. These individuals may support your accommodation requests and provide guidance through the process.

- Connect with disability employee resource groups if your company has them. These groups often provide peer support, advocacy assistance, and education for employees with disabilities.

- **Documentation Practices**

- Maintain a file containing all accommodation-related documents: your initial request, medical documentation, communications with HR and supervisors, notes from meetings about accommodations, documentation of approved accommodations, and any records of problems or denied requests.

- After verbal discussions about accommodations, send email summaries: "This email confirms our conversation today about my accommodation request. We discussed X, Y, and Z. My understanding is that you'll respond by [date]. Please let me know if I've misunderstood anything."

- These emails create written records of verbal discussions and confirm mutual understanding. They're not accusatory— they're simply good professional practice that happens to create documentation.

- Document accommodation effectiveness once implemented. Keep notes about how accommodations help your work performance. This documentation is useful if you need to request modifications or if you change positions.

- **When to Involve HR**

- HR serves multiple functions in accommodation processes. Understanding when HR involvement helps versus when it complicates matters guides your strategic decisions.

- **Situations Requiring HR Involvement**

- Formal accommodation requests under the ADA require HR involvement. HR manages the interactive process, reviews medical documentation, and documents approved accommodations. You can't bypass HR for formal requests.

- Discrimination complaints require HR involvement. If you believe you're experiencing discrimination based on your disability, reporting to HR creates a record and triggers the company's obligation to investigate.

- Supervisor conflicts about accommodations require HR involvement. If your supervisor denies reasonable accommodation requests or creates obstacles to approved accommodations, HR should intervene.

- **Situations Where HR Involvement May Not Help**

- Minor informal accommodations with supportive supervisors don't require HR involvement. If your supervisor agrees to let you wear headphones or work from home occasionally, you don't need to formalize this unless you want documentation.

- Personal conflicts with colleagues that don't involve discrimination don't require HR involvement. HR manages compliance and risk, not interpersonal dynamics.

- Situations where you want privacy about your disability don't require HR involvement unless you need formal accommodations. If you're managing fine with informal arrangements and don't want HR to know about your diagnosis, that's your right.

- **Working Effectively With HR**

- HR professionals vary in their understanding of disability accommodation law and their commitment to supporting disabled employees. Some HR representatives are knowledgeable and supportive. Others are primarily concerned with protecting the company from liability.

- Approach HR professionally and document all interactions. Present clear requests with supporting documentation. Focus on legal rights and business justifications rather than emotional appeals. Be persistent but professional if you encounter resistance.

- If your company's HR doesn't respond appropriately, consider external resources: EEOC complaints, disability rights organizations, or legal consultation.

- **Case Study: Yolanda's HR Partnership**

- Yolanda worked for a large healthcare organization with a sophisticated HR department. When she decided to request accommodations, she approached HR directly rather than going through her supervisor first.

- "I scheduled a meeting with an HR representative who specialized in accommodations. I brought my doctor's letter and a list of requested accommodations. I explained my situation clearly and asked for guidance through the process."

- The HR representative was knowledgeable and supportive. She explained the interactive process, helped Yolanda refine her accommodation requests to align with ADA language, and advised her on medical documentation requirements.

- "She became my ally through the process. She facilitated discussions with my supervisor, ensured my requests were taken seriously, and helped problem-solve when implementation challenges arose."

- Yolanda's accommodations included modified work hours, a private office, and exemption from certain social events. All were approved and implemented within four weeks.

- "Having HR on my side made the process much smoother. In my organization, HR genuinely supported accommodation requests. In other organizations, that might not be the case. You need to assess your specific HR department's approach."

- **Taking Action**

- Self-advocacy requires courage, especially after years of accommodating everyone else's needs while neglecting your own. But advocating for necessary accommodations isn't being difficult or demanding—it's ensuring you have equal access to employment opportunities.

- You don't need perfect language or flawless confidence to advocate effectively. You need understanding of your rights, clarity about your needs, willingness to communicate directly, and persistence when facing obstacles. Each advocacy experience builds skills that serve you throughout your career.

- The next chapter addresses how to use accommodations and other strategies to redesign your work life for sustainable success. Accommodations create the foundation. Strategic work redesign builds on that foundation to create a professional life that works with your neurology instead of against it.

- **Key Takeaways**

- **Legal Foundations**

- The ADA provides protection against employment discrimination and guarantees right to reasonable accommodations

- Reasonable accommodations are modifications allowing you to perform essential job functions

- The interactive process requires collaborative discussion between you and your employer to identify effective accommodations

- State and local laws may provide additional protections beyond federal requirements

- **Strategic Disclosure**

- Formal ADA accommodations require disclosing disability status but not specific diagnosis

- Weigh disclosure benefits (legal protection, accommodations, relief) against risks (potential discrimination, changed perceptions)

- Consider job security, company culture, supervisor relationship, and your current capacity when deciding about disclosure

- Selective disclosure—revealing to some people but not others—is a valid option

- **Effective Communication**

- Frame accommodation requests around functional impacts rather than diagnostic labels

- Be specific about needed accommodations and explain how they help you perform job functions

- Use clear "need" language rather than tentative requests suggesting accommodations are optional

- Document all accommodation discussions and follow up verbal conversations with written summaries

- **Common Accommodations**

- Sensory accommodations address lighting, noise, temperature, and workspace location

- Communication accommodations include written materials, advance notice, and alternative participation methods

- Schedule accommodations involve flexibility, remote work, and advance notice of changes

- Meeting accommodations reduce attendance requirements and provide alternative participation options

- **Handling Challenges**

- Respond to pushback with education about ADA requirements and clear documentation

- File internal complaints if informal resolution fails

- Use EEOC complaints and legal consultation when employers violate accommodation rights

- Build alliances with supportive colleagues and HR representatives who understand disability rights

Chapter 8: Redesigning Your Work Life

- Accommodations provide necessary support, but true sustainability requires more than environmental modifications. You need comprehensive redesign of how you approach work—how you manage energy, structure tasks, communicate with others, and make career decisions. This redesign process starts with honest assessment of your current situation through an autistic lens, identifying what works and what drains you unsustainably.

- Many autistic women reach mid-career before recognizing that their struggles aren't personal failings but mismatches between their neurological processing and workplace demands. Once you understand this mismatch, you can intentionally design work structures that minimize exhaustion while maximizing your natural strengths. This chapter provides frameworks for conducting that redesign systematically.

- **Auditing Your Current Job**

- Before redesigning your work life, assess your current situation honestly. What aspects of your job energize you versus drain you? Which tasks align with your strengths? Which create disproportionate difficulty? This audit identifies specific targets for redesign.

- **Energy Mapping**

- Track your energy levels throughout typical workdays for two weeks. Note which activities deplete your energy and which restore it. Rate your energy on a simple scale—high, medium, low—at regular intervals. Document what you're doing when energy drops sharply.

- You'll likely notice patterns. Certain types of tasks consistently drain energy while others maintain or restore it. Some environmental conditions correlate with rapid energy depletion. Specific times of day show characteristic energy patterns.

- This mapping reveals where redesign efforts should focus. If meetings consistently deplete your energy severely, meeting reduction becomes a priority. If afternoons show dramatic energy decline, schedule restructuring might help. If certain colleagues' communication styles exhaust you, boundary-setting with those individuals becomes necessary.

- **Strength and Challenge Identification**

- List tasks you perform regularly. For each task, note if it aligns with your strengths or requires significant compensatory effort. Autistic strengths often include pattern recognition, detailed analysis, systematic thinking, focused concentration, and independent work. Challenges often involve ambiguous tasks, rapid context-switching, extensive verbal communication, and unstructured social interaction.

- Tasks aligning with strengths shouldn't drain you excessively. If they do, environmental factors or insufficient recovery time may be the problem rather than the tasks themselves. Tasks requiring constant compensation will always drain energy disproportionately.

- Ideally, you spend most of your time on strength-aligned tasks and minimal time on challenge-heavy tasks. Reality rarely matches this ideal, but understanding the current distribution helps identify redesign opportunities.

- **Role Clarity Assessment**

142

- Evaluate how clearly your role is defined. Clear roles with explicit expectations suit many autistic people well. Ambiguous roles requiring constant interpretation of unspoken expectations create unnecessary difficulty.

- Do you understand what's expected of you? Do you receive clear feedback about your performance? Do you know which tasks are essential versus peripheral? If you're constantly uncertain about expectations, role clarification should be a redesign priority.

- **Case Study: Bethany's Work Audit Revelations**

- Bethany worked as a project coordinator. She felt constantly overwhelmed and questioned if she was suited for the role. After her autism diagnosis, she conducted a thorough work audit.

- "I tracked my energy for three weeks. The patterns were striking. Solo work on project documentation energized me. Meetings drained me severely. Client calls exhausted me more than internal meetings. Mornings were my peak productivity time but I was wasting them on low-priority tasks."

- Bethany also analyzed which tasks aligned with her strengths versus which required extensive compensation. "Planning, organizing, and documenting projects used my natural strengths. Facilitating group discussions, managing interpersonal conflicts, and reading subtle client cues all required exhausting compensation."

- Her role included significant time on compensation-heavy tasks. "I was spending 60% of my time on activities that drained me excessively and only 40% on activities that used my strengths. No wonder I was exhausted constantly."

- The audit revealed that Bethany was well-suited for many aspects of project coordination but poorly suited for the interpersonal facilitation components. "I wasn't failing at my job. My job included components that would exhaust any autistic person. I needed to restructure, not try harder."

- **Energy Management Strategies**

- Understanding your energy patterns allows strategic management rather than reactive coping. Effective energy management involves working with your natural rhythms, building in recovery time, and protecting your peak productivity periods.

- **Working With Your Chronotype**

- Some autistic people function best in mornings. Others peak in late afternoon or evening. Many neurotypical work schedules assume morning peak productivity, but this doesn't match everyone's natural rhythm.

- If possible, schedule demanding cognitive work during your peak energy times. Save routine, low-demand tasks for low-energy periods. If you can't control your schedule fully, at least protect peak times from energy-draining activities like back-to-back meetings.

- Advocate for schedule flexibility if your chronotype doesn't match standard work hours. "I'm most productive in the afternoon. Could I work 11-7 instead of 9-5?" presents a reasonable request if your role allows flexibility.

- **The Recovery Time Formula**

- Different activities require different recovery times. Intense social interaction might need 30 minutes of solitude for every 10 minutes of interaction. Sensory-challenging environments might need 15 minutes of recovery per hour of exposure. Deep focus work might require breaks every 90 minutes.

- Identify your personal recovery ratios. How much recovery time do you need after meetings? After client calls? After working in overstimulating environments? Build this recovery

144

time into your schedule rather than trying to power through continuously.

- If your role doesn't allow sufficient recovery time, redesign becomes necessary. You might reduce meeting attendance, transition to more remote work, or restructure your day to include adequate breaks.

- **Energy Budgeting**

- Treat energy like money in a budget. You have a finite amount available. You choose how to spend it. Some expenditures are necessary. Others are discretionary. The goal is spending wisely to maximize what matters while minimizing waste.

- Identify your daily energy capacity realistically. What can you actually sustain long-term, not what you've pushed yourself to achieve short-term? That sustainable capacity is your budget.

- List your energy expenditures: required work tasks, necessary personal maintenance, and optional activities. If your required expenditures exceed your budget, you're operating unsustainably. Something must change—either increasing income (through accommodations that reduce energy costs) or reducing expenditures (through task modification or elimination).

- **Case Study: Theresa's Schedule Redesign**

- Theresa worked as a financial analyst. Her typical schedule included scattered meetings throughout the day, fragmenting her time into useless chunks. She was constantly exhausted and behind on analytical work.

- "After auditing my energy patterns, I realized the fragmented schedule was destroying my productivity. I needed blocks of uninterrupted time for analysis, but I was getting 30-minute chunks between meetings. By the time I focused on a task, another meeting interrupted."

- Theresa proposed a schedule redesign to her supervisor: consolidating meetings into two afternoon blocks on Tuesdays and Thursdays, leaving mornings and other days meeting-free for concentrated analytical work.

- "My supervisor initially resisted—he wanted flexibility to schedule meetings whenever. I explained that the current schedule was preventing me from completing analytical work effectively. I showed data on how much time I was losing to context-switching and how consolidating meetings would improve my productivity."

- Her supervisor agreed to a trial period. Theresa's productivity increased dramatically. She completed analyses faster and with better quality. Her exhaustion decreased because she had adequate recovery time built into her schedule.

- "The meeting consolidation changed everything. I wasn't working more hours. I was working with my brain's natural functioning instead of against it. That made all the difference."

- **Optimizing Your Environment**

- Your physical environment significantly affects your functioning. Even in shared spaces, you have more control than you might realize. Strategic environmental optimization reduces sensory drain and supports concentration.

- **Lighting Modifications**

- Replace or disable fluorescent lights if possible. Use desk lamps with warm LED bulbs. Position your workspace to maximize natural light if you find it comfortable or minimize it if it creates glare.

- If you can't modify overhead lighting, use computer screen filters to reduce blue light. Wear tinted glasses if they help. Position your monitor to minimize reflection from overhead lights.

- **Sound Management**

- Noise-canceling headphones block distracting sounds. White noise or ambient sound apps can mask background conversation. Earplugs provide another option if headphones are uncomfortable.

- If your workspace is in a noisy area, request relocation to a quieter spot. Position yourself away from high-traffic areas, printers, coffee machines, and break rooms.

- For home offices, soundproofing options include acoustic panels, heavy curtains, door sweeps, and strategic furniture placement.

- **Visual Organization**

- Visual clutter creates cognitive load. Organize your workspace to minimize visual distraction. Use drawer storage instead of open shelving. Keep only current projects visible. Create simple, consistent organizational systems.

- If you work in a shared space with visual chaos beyond your control, create a small area you can control—your immediate desk space—and make it as calm as possible.

- **Temperature Control**

- Temperature sensitivity varies individually. Some autistic people are extremely sensitive to being too hot or too cold. Inability to control temperature creates constant distress.

- Request control over your immediate environment's temperature if possible. Use personal fans, space heaters (if permitted), or heated/cooling pads. Dress in layers so you can adjust.

- If building temperature control is inflexible, advocate for accommodation. Medical documentation of temperature sensitivity can support requests for workspace relocation or personal heating/cooling devices.

- **Communication Systems That Work**

- Neurotypical workplaces often favor verbal, synchronous communication. Autistic people often communicate more effectively through written, asynchronous formats. Redesigning your communication systems to favor formats that work with your processing style reduces exhaustion and improves quality.

- **Preferring Written Communication**

- Written communication allows processing time. You can read, think, formulate responses carefully, and communicate clearly without real-time pressure. Email, messaging apps, and shared documents support this communication style.

- Establish written communication as your default. "I process information better in writing. Could you send me an email about that instead of explaining verbally?" This simple request often gets accepted without issue.

- For complex discussions, propose asynchronous written exchange instead of meetings. "Let me write up my thoughts on this and share them with you. You can respond in writing and we can discuss remaining questions."

- **Meeting Participation Strategies**

- If you must attend meetings, implement strategies to make participation less draining. Request agendas in advance so you can prepare. Take notes to help focus attention. Request follow-up summaries of key decisions.

- Participate strategically rather than constantly. You don't need to contribute to every discussion. Prepare one or two key points and deliver them. This focused participation often proves more effective than trying to engage continuously.

- For video meetings, turn off self-view to reduce cognitive load. Use chat features to contribute in writing when verbal participation feels overwhelming.

- **Setting Communication Boundaries**

- Establish boundaries about communication methods and timing. "I don't take phone calls without advance notice. Please email me to schedule a call." This boundary protects you from unexpected verbal communication that interrupts focus.

- Set work hour boundaries if possible. "I respond to emails during work hours. I don't check email in evenings or weekends." This protects recovery time.

- Use out-of-office messages liberally. "I'm focusing on a deadline today and won't be checking email regularly. For urgent matters, contact [alternative person]." This creates space for deep work without constant interruption.

- **Case Study: Nora's Communication Revolution**

- Nora worked as a technical support specialist. Her job involved constant phone calls from frustrated customers—one of the most draining activities possible for her. She was burning out rapidly.

- "Every call required extensive social processing on top of technical problem-solving. I was exhausting myself on phone support while having little energy left for the technical work I actually enjoyed."

- After her autism diagnosis, Nora proposed restructuring her role. "I asked to transition from phone support to technical documentation and email support. I would write help guides, improve documentation, and respond to customer emails instead of taking calls."

- Her manager was initially skeptical—phone support was considered essential. But Nora demonstrated how email support could be equally effective for many customer issues while being more efficient.

- "I showed data that many customer problems could be resolved with better documentation and that email support allowed customers to describe issues clearly, giving me time to research and provide thorough solutions."

- The company agreed to a modified role. Nora's job satisfaction increased dramatically. Her burnout symptoms decreased. The company gained high-quality technical documentation and effective email support.

- "I wasn't refusing to help customers. I was finding a way to help them effectively using communication methods that worked with my brain instead of against it."

- **Time Blocking and Routines**

- Predictability and structure support autistic functioning. Time blocking and established routines reduce cognitive load from constant decision-making and provide the predictability that allows effective work.

- **The Time Blocking Method**

- Time blocking assigns specific time blocks to specific activities. Instead of fluid schedules where you decide moment-by-moment what to work on, you schedule focused blocks for different work types.

- Typical time blocking might include: 9-11 AM deep analytical work, 11-11:30 email processing, 11:30-12 administrative tasks, 1-2 PM meetings, 2-4 PM project work, 4-4:30 planning next day.

- The structure reduces decision fatigue. You know what you're doing at any given time without constant decision-making

150

about priorities. The predictability also supports focus—you're not wondering if you should be doing something else instead.

- **Building Sustainable Routines**

- Routines reduce cognitive load and create structure. Morning routines prepare you for work without requiring decisions. Work routines create predictable patterns. Evening routines support transition from work to rest.

- Autistic people often develop elaborate routines naturally. Use this tendency productively by creating routines that support sustainable functioning rather than just compensating for poor work structure.

- Your routines should include recovery time, not just productive work. A sustainable routine might be: 30 minutes planning, 90 minutes focused work, 15 minutes recovery, 90 minutes focused work, 30 minutes lunch break, 60 minutes communication tasks, 30 minutes recovery, 90 minutes focused work, 30 minutes planning next day.

- **Protecting Your Systems**

- Once you establish effective routines and time blocking, protect them from constant disruption. "I have focused work blocks scheduled and can't take a meeting then. I'm available during these times instead." This boundary protection maintains the system's effectiveness.

- Some flexibility is necessary—emergencies happen, urgent issues arise. But most schedule requests aren't actually urgent. Defaulting to protecting your system while accommodating genuine urgency maintains sustainability.

- **Technology Tools and Solutions**

- Technology can support autistic functioning in workplace contexts. Strategic tool use reduces cognitive load, improves organization, and compensates for executive function challenges.

- **Task Management Systems**

- Project management apps, to-do list systems, and calendar apps externalize task tracking. Instead of keeping everything in working memory, you capture tasks in reliable systems.

- Choose systems that match your thinking style. Some autistic people prefer detailed hierarchical systems. Others work better with simple linear lists. Some need visual boards. Others prefer text-based systems.

- The specific tool matters less than consistent use. Find a system that works for your brain and use it consistently. Resist constantly switching systems—that creates more work than it saves.

- **Communication Management**

- Email filters and folders automatically sort incoming messages, reducing cognitive load from constant inbox processing. Templates for common communications save time and reduce the burden of formulating responses repeatedly.

- Text expansion tools automatically insert frequently used phrases. Calendar tools with automatic meeting scheduling reduce back-and-forth about finding times. Video meeting platforms with recordings allow you to review discussions instead of processing everything in real-time.

- **Focus and Attention Support**

- Website blockers prevent distraction during focused work. Pomodoro timer apps structure work and break time. White noise or ambient sound apps mask distracting environmental noise. Distraction-free writing apps minimize visual clutter and interface distractions.

- Screen time tracking apps provide data on where your time actually goes, helping identify time leaks and unproductive patterns.

- **Executive Function Support**

- Reminder systems prompt you for time-based tasks. Automated workflows handle repetitive processes. Integration between tools reduces the cognitive load of manually transferring information between systems.

- Voice recording apps capture ideas during meetings or conversations, allowing you to review them later rather than processing everything in real-time.

- **Case Study: Shanice's Technology Stack**

- Shanice worked as a UX designer. She struggled with task management and executive function until she developed a technology system that supported her processing style.

- "I was constantly forgetting tasks, missing deadlines, and feeling overwhelmed by everything I needed to track. I tried various to-do list apps but nothing stuck until I found a system that matched how my brain works."

- Shanice's system combined several tools working together: a project management app for work tasks with detailed subtasks and deadlines, a calendar synced across devices with color-coding for different activity types, email filters automatically sorting messages into folders, and templates for common responses.

- "The system externalizes everything I'd been trying to hold in my head. Tasks are captured in the project management app. Appointments are in my calendar with automated reminders. Emails are automatically sorted so I'm not processing hundreds of messages daily."

- Shanice also uses focus tools: website blocker during deep work sessions, white noise app to mask office sounds, and distraction-free writing mode in her design software.

- "The technology stack reduced my cognitive load enormously. I'm not trying to remember everything or constantly processing incoming information. The tools handle the routine processing, freeing my brain for actual design work."

- **Building a Sustainable Schedule**

- A sustainable schedule matches your capacity, includes adequate recovery time, protects your energy for highest-priority work, and maintains boundaries that prevent overextension.

- **Capacity-Based Scheduling**

- Instead of scheduling based on what you think you should be able to do or what neurotypical colleagues manage, schedule based on your actual capacity. If you can manage four focused work hours daily sustainably, build your schedule around four hours, not eight.

- This might seem like admitting limitation, but it's actually strategic capacity recognition. Working four sustainable hours produces better results than pushing for eight unsustainable hours that lead to burnout.

- You might need to negotiate reduced hours or restructured roles to match your capacity. This negotiation is reasonable accommodation territory if your capacity limits relate to your disability.

- **Strategic Priority Placement**

- Schedule your highest-priority, most demanding work during peak energy times. Save lower-priority, less demanding tasks for low-energy periods. Protect peak times from energy-draining activities like meetings or low-value communication tasks.

- If meetings must occur, schedule them during low-energy times when you couldn't do demanding work anyway. This maximizes value from your peak energy.

- **Recovery Time Integration**

- Recovery time isn't optional—it's necessary for sustainable functioning. Schedule recovery time explicitly: breaks between meetings, quiet time after social interaction, decompression time after sensory challenges.

- Treat recovery time as sacred as work time. It's not time you're wasting—it's maintenance necessary for continued functioning.

- **Saying No to Protect Your Schedule**

- The most sustainable schedule fails if you constantly agree to additions that exceed your capacity. Saying no protects your carefully designed schedule from erosion.

- "I don't have capacity for that right now" is a complete sentence. You don't need elaborate justifications. If pressed, "Taking that on would compromise my existing commitments" explains without apologizing.

- **Career Pivots and Transitions**

- Sometimes redesign within your current role isn't sufficient. The fundamental nature of the job might not match your strengths. The industry might have cultural norms incompatible with autistic functioning. The specific company might lack support for neurodivergent employees. Strategic career pivots might serve you better than continued adaptation to unsuitable situations.

-

- **Recognizing When Redesign Isn't Enough**

- If you've implemented accommodations, optimized your environment, redesigned your schedule, and improved communication systems but still struggle unsustainably, the problem might be the role itself. Some jobs fundamentally don't match autistic processing styles.

- Jobs requiring constant rapid context-switching, extensive ambiguous social interaction, high sensory demands in non-modifiable environments, or core tasks that drain you despite accommodations might simply not be good fits.

- This doesn't mean you're failing. It means you've identified a poor match between your strengths and the role's demands. Finding a better match represents strategic career management, not defeat.

- **Identifying Better-Fit Roles**

- Better-fit roles typically emphasize your strengths, minimize your most challenging activities, provide clear expectations, allow meaningful control over environment and schedule, and exist within organizations supportive of neurodivergent employees.

- Consider roles emphasizing: deep analysis over social facilitation, written over verbal communication, independent over group work, predictable over constantly changing demands, and clear over ambiguous expectations.

- Also consider work arrangements: remote work, self-employment, contract/freelance work, part-time roles, or positions in neurodiversity-focused organizations.

- **Planning Strategic Transitions**

- Career transitions work best when planned strategically rather than made impulsively during burnout crisis. Identify your target role or direction. Research requirements and typical

156

paths. Develop necessary skills or credentials. Build financial reserves to support transition. Network in your target area.

- Transition gradually if possible. Stay in your current role while building toward the new direction. This provides financial stability and reduces pressure during the transition.

- **Case Study: Lena's Career Pivot**

- Lena worked in marketing for a large consumer goods company. The job required extensive client interaction, frequent travel, and constant adaptation to changing campaigns. Despite accommodations and personal redesign efforts, she couldn't make it sustainable.

- "I'd implemented every strategy I could think of. I had accommodations. I'd optimized my schedule. I used all the tools and techniques. But the fundamental nature of the work—constant social performance, rapid changes, high sensory demands—didn't match my processing style."

- Lena recognized she needed a career change, not just job modifications. She'd always been interested in data analysis and had strong analytical skills. She researched data analyst roles and found they emphasized analysis over social performance, solitary over collaborative work, and predictable over rapidly changing demands.

- "I enrolled in online data analysis courses while keeping my marketing job. I completed a certification program over ten months. I built a portfolio of analysis projects. I networked with data analysts through professional associations."

- After a year of preparation, Lena transitioned to a data analyst role at a different company. The new role suited her strengths far better. Her stress decreased dramatically. Her work satisfaction increased.

- "The career change wasn't about the marketing industry being wrong for autistic people. It was about that specific type of marketing role being wrong for my specific profile. Data analysis uses my analytical strengths without requiring constant social performance. It's a better match for how my brain works."

- **Moving Forward With Purpose**

- Redesigning your work life is ongoing rather than a one-time project. Your needs change. Work demands change. You gain new insights about what works and what doesn't. Effective redesign involves regular reassessment and adjustment.

- The goal isn't achieving perfect sustainability immediately. The goal is moving toward increasingly sustainable patterns while accepting that some trial and error is necessary. Each redesign iteration teaches you more about your needs and effective strategies.

- The next chapter addresses building support systems beyond your individual efforts. Work redesign combined with strong support networks creates the conditions for long-term professional thriving.

- **Key Takeaways**

- **Assessment Foundations**

- Energy mapping reveals which activities drain versus restore you

- Strength and challenge identification shows where compensation is necessary versus where you're working naturally

- Regular work audits identify specific targets for redesign efforts

- Honest capacity assessment prevents unsustainable scheduling

- **Energy Management**

- Work with your natural chronotype rather than forcing incompatible schedules

- Calculate recovery time needed for different activities and build it into schedules

- Budget energy like money, tracking expenditures and ensuring income matches expenses

- Protect peak energy times for highest-priority work

- **Environmental Optimization**

- Modify lighting, sound, and temperature within your control

- Use tools like headphones, desk lamps, and personal climate control devices

- Organize your immediate workspace even if you can't control shared spaces

- Request accommodations for environmental factors beyond your control

- **Communication Redesign**

- Favor written, asynchronous communication over verbal, synchronous when possible

- Set boundaries about communication methods and response times

- Use meeting participation strategies to reduce cognitive load

- Establish your preferred communication style as default rather than exception

- **Structure and Systems**

- Time blocking reduces decision fatigue and provides predictability

- Routines decrease cognitive load for repetitive activities

- Technology tools externalize task tracking and executive function demands

- Protect established systems from constant disruption while maintaining necessary flexibility

- **Career Development**

- Some roles fundamentally don't match autistic processing styles despite accommodations

- Strategic career pivots to better-fit roles support long-term sustainability

- Plan transitions carefully with skill development and financial preparation

- Better-fit roles emphasize your strengths and minimize most challenging activities

Chapter 9: Building Your Support Ecosystem

- Professional success doesn't happen in isolation. The autistic woman navigating workplace challenges needs support systems that provide understanding, practical assistance, and genuine connection. These support systems differ from traditional professional networking—they prioritize authenticity over performance, understanding over sympathy, and practical problem-solving over motivational platitudes.

- Building your support ecosystem requires strategic effort. You need to identify people who understand autistic experiences, create relationships based on genuine reciprocity, and establish both personal and professional support structures. This chapter provides frameworks for building the support systems that sustain long-term professional thriving.

- **Finding Your Neurodivergent Community**

- Connection with other neurodivergent people—particularly other autistic women—provides validation, practical advice, and the relief of being understood without translation. These connections can happen online or in person, through formal organizations or informal networks.

- **The Value of Shared Experience**

- Other autistic people understand experiences you've struggled to explain to neurotypical friends and family. They don't need explanations about sensory overload, masking exhaustion, or communication differences. They recognize these experiences immediately because they live them too.

- This shared understanding reduces isolation. You're not the only one who finds basic activities exhausting. You're not broken or defective. You're autistic, and other autistic people experience similar challenges.

- Neurodivergent communities also provide practical knowledge. People share accommodation strategies that worked for them, workplace scripts that succeeded, burnout recovery approaches, and career paths that suit autistic processing styles. This collective wisdom saves you from reinventing solutions others have already discovered.

- **Online Communities**

- Online autistic communities exist on multiple platforms: Reddit forums, Facebook groups, Discord servers, Twitter communities, and dedicated websites. These communities allow connection regardless of geographic location.

- Online communities offer advantages: accessibility from home, asynchronous participation allowing processing time, ability to lurk and observe before participating, and connections with diverse autistic people beyond your immediate area.

- Look for communities specifically for autistic women or autistic adults. General autism communities often center children's autism or male experiences. Communities for autistic women provide more relevant discussion and support.

- Evaluate community culture before fully engaging. Healthy communities support members, share practical information, and maintain respectful discussion norms. Unhealthy communities might be dominated by negativity, promote harmful advice, or lack appropriate moderation.

- **In-Person Connections**

- Local autistic support groups, neurodiversity meetups, or autism-focused social groups provide in-person connection. These groups often meet monthly and offer structured activities reducing social pressure.

- In-person connection offers advantages that online interaction doesn't: direct sensory experience of others' presence, non-verbal communication, and activity-based interaction (like parallel play at craft groups) that doesn't require constant verbal engagement.

- Finding local groups requires research. Search for autism support groups in your area. Check disability services organizations. Look for neurodiversity employee resource groups at large employers. Ask autism-informed therapists about local resources.

- **Case Study: Quinn's Online Community Discovery**

- Quinn felt isolated after her autism diagnosis at 38. She didn't know any other autistic adults personally. Her neurotypical friends tried to be supportive but didn't truly understand her experiences.

- "I found an online community for late-diagnosed autistic women. Reading other women's stories was revelatory. Every post described experiences I'd thought were unique to me. The exhaustion from socializing. The confusion about unwritten social rules. The burnout patterns. Other women were living my exact experiences."

- Quinn lurked in the community for several months before posting. "I needed to observe and understand the culture. I wanted to make sure it felt safe. Once I was comfortable, I started participating."

- The community became Quinn's primary source of autism-specific support. "I could ask questions without judgment. 'Does anyone else find phone calls physically painful?'

163

generated dozens of responses from women saying yes, describing their experiences, and sharing coping strategies."

- The community also connected Quinn with other autistic professional women. "I found a subgroup focused on workplace challenges. We shared accommodation strategies, discussed disclosure decisions, and supported each other through difficult work situations. Having people who understood both autism and professional life was invaluable."

- **Case Study: Delia's Local Group Connection**

- Delia preferred in-person connection to online interaction. She searched for local autistic adult groups and found a monthly meetup at a community center.

- "The first meeting was nerve-wracking. I worried about being visibly awkward or not fitting in. But the moment I walked in, I felt different from any other social situation I'd experienced. People were stimming openly. Conversation was direct. No one made small talk. It felt like coming home."

- The group structure helped Delia. "We'd meet for two hours. The first hour was structured discussion on a chosen topic— workplace accommodations, burnout recovery, managing relationships. The second hour was unstructured social time with optional activities like puzzles or coloring. The structure provided conversational scaffolding without forcing constant socializing."

- Delia formed several close friendships through the group. "I met other autistic professional women who understood my workplace challenges. We started meeting separately for lunch and supported each other through difficult periods. These friendships have been more sustaining than any I've had with neurotypical people because there's no masking required."

-

- **Working With Autism-Informed Professionals**

- Therapists, coaches, and other helping professionals who understand autism can provide specialized support. However, finding professionals with genuine autism competence— particularly for adult autistic women—requires careful vetting.

- **Identifying Autism-Informed Therapists**

- Autism-informed therapists understand autistic processing styles, recognize masking and burnout, validate autistic experiences rather than pathologizing them, and work collaboratively rather than imposing neurotypical norms.

- Look for therapists who explicitly list autism in their specialties for adults, not just children. Ask about their approach: Do they work with autistic adults regularly? Do they understand the female autism phenotype? Do they recognize masking and its costs? Do they support acceptance rather than forcing change toward neurotypical presentation?

- Red flags include therapists who focus primarily on making you more neurotypical, who dismiss your self-diagnosis or insist on formal assessment they provide, who don't understand masking, or who suggest your autistic traits need fixing.

- **Career Coaches and Vocational Support**

- Career coaches who understand neurodiversity can help with job searches, career transitions, workplace accommodations, and professional development from a neurodivergent-affirming perspective.

- Standard career coaches often provide advice that doesn't work for autistic people: "Network extensively at large events!" "Always maintain eye contact during interviews!" "Be flexible and adapt to whatever your employer needs!"

Neurodiversity-informed coaches understand why standard advice fails and provide alternatives.

- Look for coaches with neurodiversity specialization or experience working with autistic clients. Ask about their approach to accommodations, their understanding of autistic strengths, and their strategies for managing workplace challenges specific to neurodivergent professionals.

- **Medical and Psychiatric Support**

- Psychiatrists and physicians who understand autism provide better mental health treatment. They recognize that anxiety and depression in autistic adults often stem from environmental mismatch and masking exhaustion, not just chemical imbalances.

- Autism-informed psychiatrists prescribe medication when appropriate but also address environmental factors and burnout. They understand that SSRIs might help depression but won't resolve depression caused by unsustainable masking demands.

- Finding these professionals requires research. Ask for recommendations in autistic communities. Check professional directories for autism specialization. Interview potential providers about their experience with autistic adults before committing.

- **Case Study: Morgan's Therapeutic Partnership**

- Morgan tried several therapists after her autism diagnosis. Her first therapist focused on teaching social skills and changing Morgan's communication style—essentially encouraging more masking. This approach made things worse.

- "She kept suggesting I should try harder to read people's emotions, practice making more eye contact, and force myself to attend more social events. She didn't understand that I'd

166

been trying those things for decades and that they were exhausting me."

- Morgan switched to a therapist who specialized in autism in adults. "The difference was immediate. She understood masking. She validated my experiences. She didn't try to make me more neurotypical. Instead, she helped me figure out how to live authentically while managing necessary accommodations to neurotypical environments."

- The autism-informed therapist helped Morgan process trauma from years of misunderstanding, develop strategies for sustainable work life, and build self-acceptance. "She helped me understand that I wasn't broken or deficient. I was autistic, and autism isn't something to fix. The goal was helping me thrive as an autistic person, not trying to make me neurotypical."

- **Educating Partners and Family**

- Close personal relationships require education about autism for mutual understanding and support. Partners, family members, and close friends need to understand how autism affects you, what you need, and how they can provide effective support.

- **Starting the Conversation**

- Begin by sharing your diagnosis and what it means for you specifically. Avoid assuming people understand autism—most have stereotypical or outdated knowledge. Provide education through resources you've found helpful: books by autistic authors, articles about autism in women, videos by autistic advocates.

- Explain your specific needs clearly. "I need quiet time alone after social events to recover from sensory and social demands." "I communicate better in writing for important

167

discussions." "I need advance notice for changes to plans." Specific information helps people provide effective support.

- Discuss masking and its costs. Help loved ones understand that you may present differently in private than in public, that the difference reflects exhaustion from masking rather than deception, and that you need safe spaces where masking isn't necessary.

- **Common Education Challenges**

- Some family members resist your autism identity. "You're not autistic—you're just shy!" "Everyone feels overwhelmed sometimes." "You're using autism as an excuse." These responses invalidate your experiences and demonstrate lack of understanding.

- Respond firmly but calmly. "I've been diagnosed by a professional who specializes in autism in adults. My experiences match autistic patterns clearly. I need you to accept my autism even if you don't fully understand it."

- Provide written resources for people who need time to process information. "I know this is new information. Here are some articles that explain autism in women. Please read them and we can discuss questions you have."

- Some people never accept your autism. This is painful, but continuing to argue rarely helps. Focus energy on relationships with people who do accept and support you.

- **Building Reciprocal Understanding**

- Education shouldn't be one-sided. Ask loved ones what they need from you. Your autism affects your relationships, and while you shouldn't apologize for being autistic, you should maintain awareness of how your needs interact with others' needs.

- Negotiate accommodations in relationships just as you do at work. "I need advance notice for social plans. In return, once I commit, I'll follow through reliably." "I need you to communicate clearly and directly instead of hinting. In return, I'll work on not taking direct communication as criticism."

- **Case Study: Irene's Partner Education Process**

- Irene's partner of five years initially struggled to understand her autism diagnosis. He'd seen her mask in public and didn't recognize the exhaustion it caused her or how differently she functioned in private.

- "He said, 'But you're so good with people at parties!' He didn't see that I was performing, that it exhausted me, and that I needed days to recover afterward. He thought my need for alone time was rejection of him rather than necessary recovery."

- Irene shared articles and videos about autism in women, focusing particularly on masking. She explained her specific experiences in detail. "I showed him my energy logs—how my energy dropped dramatically after social events, how I needed quiet time to recover, how masking at work meant I had nothing left for home life."

- Gradually, her partner developed understanding. "He started recognizing my masking. He noticed when I was forcing myself to be social. He began respecting my need for recovery time without taking it personally."

- They negotiated accommodations in their relationship. Irene needed advance notice for plans, quiet time after work before social interaction, and direct communication rather than hints or implications. Her partner needed Irene to communicate when she was overwhelmed rather than just withdrawing, to maintain certain shared activities even when tired, and to appreciate his efforts to understand and accommodate.

- "The relationship improved significantly once we both understood how autism affected our interactions. He provides better support because he understands my needs. I'm better at communicating my needs clearly instead of expecting him to guess."

- **Workplace Mentors and Allies**

- Professional support within your workplace provides practical assistance with career navigation, political dynamics, and day-to-day challenges. These workplace allies might be mentors, supportive colleagues, or understanding supervisors.

- **Identifying Potential Allies**

- Workplace allies demonstrate several characteristics: they respect different work styles, they've advocated for others or themselves, they show genuine interest in equity and inclusion, and they maintain confidentiality when needed.

- Look for people who've mentioned neurodiversity positively, who've requested accommodations themselves, who've supported colleagues through difficulties, or who actively participate in diversity initiatives.

- Observe how potential allies respond to difference. Do they react with curiosity or judgment when someone does things differently? Do they support or criticize colleagues who need accommodations? Do they value diverse approaches or insist on conformity?

- **Building Mentorship Relationships**

- Formal mentorship programs within companies can connect you with experienced professionals who provide career guidance. Informal mentorship develops through building relationships with people whose experience and approach you value.

- Be clear about what you need from mentorship. Guidance about career advancement? Help navigating office politics? Technical skill development? Understanding what you need helps you find appropriate mentors and communicate expectations.

- Reciprocate in mentorship relationships. Offer your expertise, provide support, and contribute value. Healthy mentorship involves mutual benefit even if the relationship isn't perfectly equal.

- **Leveraging Employee Resource Groups**

- Disability employee resource groups (ERGs) provide community, advocacy, and support within organizations. These groups often include neurodivergent members and allies who understand disability-related workplace challenges.

- ERGs can provide peer support, educate the organization about disability inclusion, advocate for policy changes, and connect you with others navigating similar challenges. Join your organization's disability ERG if one exists. If not, consider working with others to create one.

- **Case Study: Autumn's Mentor Network**

- Autumn worked as an engineer at a large aerospace company. After disclosing her autism and requesting accommodations, she felt isolated—her immediate team was supportive but didn't understand neurodiversity deeply.

- "I joined the company's disability ERG. There I met other neurodivergent employees who understood my experiences. I connected with a senior engineer who was openly autistic and who became an informal mentor."

- Her mentor provided practical advice about navigating the company's culture as an autistic employee. "He explained which managers were neurodiversity-friendly, which projects suited autistic engineers, and how to request accommodations effectively. He also shared his own experiences—the mistakes he'd made, the strategies that worked, and how he'd built a successful career while autistic."

- Autumn also connected with a manager in a different department who advocated for neurodiversity inclusion. "She wasn't autistic but was deeply committed to disability inclusion. She became an ally who helped me navigate political situations I didn't understand and who advocated for me in contexts where I didn't have access."

- The combination of peer support from other neurodivergent employees, mentorship from someone with shared lived experience, and advocacy from a neurotypical ally created a strong support network. "I wasn't alone anymore. I had people who understood my challenges, who could provide advice, and who would support me when difficulties arose."

- **Professional Networks That Celebrate Neurodiversity**

- Beyond individual workplace relationships, professional networks focused on neurodiversity provide broader community and career resources. These networks exist both within specific industries and across professional fields.

- **Neurodiversity-Focused Professional Organizations**

- Several organizations focus specifically on neurodivergent professionals: Autistic Self Advocacy Network (ASAN) has resources for autistic professionals. Neurodiversity in the Workplace groups exist in many cities. Industry-specific neurodiversity groups are emerging in tech, finance, healthcare, and other fields.

- These organizations provide networking events, professional development, job boards, mentorship matching, and advocacy for workplace inclusion. Membership connects you with other neurodivergent professionals and with employers actively seeking neurodivergent talent.

- **Online Professional Communities**

- LinkedIn groups, professional forums, and industry-specific online communities increasingly include neurodiversity-focused subgroups. These communities allow networking, knowledge sharing, and professional support with others who understand autism-related workplace challenges.

- Online professional communities offer accessibility advantages over in-person networking events. You can participate asynchronously, communicate in writing, and connect without the sensory and social demands of traditional networking.

- **Building Your Professional Reputation**

- Your professional network should recognize your expertise and contributions, not just your accommodation needs. Building reputation involves sharing your knowledge, contributing to professional discussions, and demonstrating your capabilities clearly.

- Being open about autism while also showcasing your professional strengths creates balanced professional identity. You're not just "the autistic employee"—you're "the brilliant data analyst who's also autistic."

- **Seeking Intensive Support During Crisis**

- Sometimes the standard support systems aren't sufficient. During burnout, mental health crisis, or major life transitions, you might need more intensive support than friends, family, and workplace allies can provide.

- **Recognizing When You Need More Support**

- Warning signs that you need intensive support include: persistent thoughts of self-harm or suicide, complete inability to function at work or home, severe burnout that doesn't improve with rest, breakdown of all coping strategies, or major life crises coinciding with autistic burnout.

- These situations require professional intervention, not just peer support. Don't wait until you're in complete crisis before seeking help.

- **Types of Intensive Support**

- Options for intensive support include intensive outpatient programs for mental health treatment, short-term disability leave with structured recovery plan, residential treatment if needed for severe mental health crisis, regular appointments with autism-informed therapists, and targeted support from occupational therapists or autism specialists.

- Medical leave from work might be necessary during severe burnout or mental health crisis. Use this time for actual recovery with professional support, not just rest at home.

- **Crisis Resources**

- If you're experiencing suicidal thoughts, call the National Suicide Prevention Lifeline (988). Crisis text line (text HOME to 741741) provides text-based crisis support. Local mental health crisis teams offer immediate assessment and connection to services.

- Having crisis resources identified before you need them helps if crisis occurs. Save these numbers in your phone. Share them with trusted friends or family who can help if you're in crisis.

- **Creating Psychological Safety**

- Beyond specific support people and resources, you need overall environments where you feel psychologically safe— able to be authentic, express needs, and trust others' responses.

Creating this safety requires intentional relationship building and boundary maintenance.

- **Safety Assessment**

- Psychologically safe relationships and environments allow you to be yourself without fear of judgment or rejection. You can express needs, make mistakes, and ask for help without negative consequences.

- Assess your current relationships and environments: Do you feel safe being authentic? Can you express needs without excessive justification? Do people respond supportively to your struggles? Can you recover from mistakes without lasting damage?

- If most of your environments lack psychological safety, prioritize building safer spaces—online communities, therapy relationships, or small friendship groups where you can be authentic.

- **Boundary Maintenance**

- Psychological safety requires boundaries. You need to limit exposure to people and situations that consistently drain you or respond negatively to your authentic self.

- Set boundaries with people who invalidate your autism, demand constant masking, or drain your energy without reciprocating support. "I need to limit our contact because these interactions are difficult for me" states a boundary clearly.

- Protect time and energy for relationships and activities that provide genuine support and connection. Saying no to draining situations creates space for nourishing ones.

- **Reciprocity Cultivation**

- Healthy support relationships involve reciprocity—both people give and receive support. One-sided relationships where you constantly support others without receiving support back aren't sustainable.

- Evaluate reciprocity in your relationships. Do people support you when you're struggling? Do they accommodate your needs as you accommodate theirs? Do they show up when you need them?

- Relationships lacking reciprocity might need boundaries or reduction. Focus energy on relationships where support flows both directions.

- **Case Study: Maya's Support System Audit**

- Maya realized at 40 that most of her relationships were one-sided. She provided extensive emotional support to friends and family but received little support for her own struggles.

- "I was the person everyone called when they had problems. I listened, provided advice, and offered practical help. But when I struggled—when I was burned out or overwhelmed—those same people were unavailable or dismissive."

- Maya conducted a relationship audit. She listed her regular relationships and assessed reciprocity, psychological safety, and energy balance for each relationship. The results were stark—most relationships drained her without providing support.

- "I had to make difficult decisions. I reduced contact with people who consistently took without giving. I let some friendships fade. I set firmer boundaries with family members who demanded my time and support but didn't reciprocate."

- Maya invested energy freed up by boundary-setting into building reciprocal relationships. She deepened connections with the few friends who did provide mutual support. She joined autistic community groups where people understood her experiences. She worked with an autism-informed therapist who helped her process the relationship changes.

- "My social network is smaller now, but much more sustaining. I have fewer relationships but better ones. The people in my life now support me genuinely, understand my autism, and maintain reciprocal relationships. Quality over quantity matters more than I'd understood."

- **Putting the Pieces Together**

- Building a support ecosystem requires ongoing effort. You need to identify people who understand your experiences, develop reciprocal relationships, establish boundaries that protect your energy, and create environments where you can be authentic. This ecosystem includes online and in-person community, professional and personal relationships, peer support and expert guidance.

- Your support needs will change over time. During periods of stability, lighter support might suffice. During crisis or major transitions, you'll need more intensive support. Building your ecosystem before crisis occurs ensures support is available when you need it.

- Professional success doesn't happen alone. Recognizing this and intentionally building supportive connections provides the foundation for long-term sustainability. Combined with self-advocacy skills and work redesign strategies, strong support systems create conditions where you can thrive professionally while remaining authentically yourself.

- **The Path You've Traveled**

- You've moved through understanding masking's exhaustion, obtaining diagnosis, recognizing how autism manifests in professional women, surviving workplace challenges, understanding burnout, practicing unmasking, advocating for accommodations, redesigning work life, and now building support systems. Each element connects to create sustainable professional life as an autistic woman.

- This isn't a linear path you complete once. It's an ongoing process of learning, adjusting, building, and growing. You'll refine your strategies, develop new skills, build stronger support networks, and create increasingly sustainable patterns. The goal isn't perfection—it's progress toward thriving rather than just surviving.

- You're not alone in this process. Thousands of autistic women are navigating similar paths, building similar support systems, and creating sustainable professional lives. You're part of a growing movement of autistic women refusing to destroy themselves for careers built on unsustainable masking demands. Together, we're creating different possibilities—for ourselves and for autistic women who come after us.

- **Key Takeaways**

- **Community Connection**

- Neurodivergent community provides validation, practical advice, and shared understanding

- Online communities offer accessibility and asynchronous participation

- In-person groups provide direct connection and activity-based interaction

- Seek communities specifically for autistic women or autistic adults for most relevant support

- **Professional Support**

- Autism-informed therapists understand masking, burnout, and autistic processing styles

- Career coaches with neurodiversity specialization provide relevant guidance

- Vet potential professionals carefully about autism competence and approach

- Red flags include focus on making you more neurotypical or dismissal of masking's costs

- **Personal Relationships**

- Partners and family need education about autism and your specific needs

- Provide clear information and resources rather than assuming understanding

- Negotiate accommodations in relationships through reciprocal discussion

- Some people may not accept your autism; focus energy on supportive relationships

- **Workplace Support**

- Identify potential allies who respect different work styles and advocate for inclusion

- Mentorship from autistic professionals or neurodiversity allies provides practical guidance

- Employee resource groups create community and advocacy within organizations

- Build professional reputation based on expertise while being open about autism

- **Intensive Support**

- Recognize signs that standard support isn't sufficient: suicidal thoughts, severe burnout, complete function loss

- Seek professional intervention during crisis: therapy, medical leave, crisis services

- Have crisis resources identified before you need them

- Medical leave may be necessary for recovery during severe burnout or mental health crisis

- **Creating Safety**

- Psychological safety allows authenticity without fear of judgment or rejection

- Assess relationships and environments for safety and reciprocity

- Set boundaries with people and situations that consistently drain or invalidate you

- Focus energy on reciprocal relationships where support flows both directions

Chapter 10: Thriving Brilliantly

The professional world has long operated on the assumption that there's one right way to think, work, and lead. This assumption has caused immense suffering for autistic women who've spent careers trying to fit a mold never designed for them. But something is shifting. Organizations are beginning—slowly, imperfectly—to recognize that cognitive diversity isn't just nice to have but necessary for innovation and excellence. Your autistic brain isn't broken or deficient. It processes information differently, and that difference creates capabilities neurotypical brains don't possess.

This final chapter focuses not on surviving but on thriving—on leveraging your autistic strengths to create meaningful professional success on your terms. You've learned to manage exhaustion, obtain accommodations, and build support systems. Now you'll discover how to position your neurological differences as the assets they actually are.

Reframing Deficits as Differences

The medical model of autism has framed autistic traits as deficits—things wrong with you that need fixing or compensating for. Social communication deficit. Restricted interests. Rigid thinking. These labels pathologize natural variations in human neurology.

The neurodiversity paradigm offers a different framework. Autism isn't deficiency—it's difference. Your brain processes information through different pathways than neurotypical brains. Sometimes this creates challenges in environments designed for neurotypical processing. But it also creates capabilities.

From Social Deficit to Communication Clarity

The diagnostic criteria describe "deficits in social communication." But many autistic women don't have communication deficits—they have different communication styles. You communicate directly, literally, and precisely. You say what you mean. You mean what you say.

In many professional contexts, this directness is an asset. Technical fields, crisis management, and leadership roles all benefit from clear, unambiguous communication. The person who says "This project will fail if we continue with the current timeline" provides more useful information than the person who hints vaguely about "concerns."

Your challenge isn't learning to communicate—it's finding environments that value your communication style.

From Restricted Interests to Deep Expertise

"Restricted, repetitive patterns of behavior, interests, or activities" sounds pathological. But what if we called it "intense focus and sustained engagement with specific domains of knowledge"? Suddenly it sounds like exactly what you need for advanced expertise.

Your special interests aren't limitations. They're the foundation for becoming genuinely excellent in your chosen field. The neurotypical person who dabbles in many topics might have breadth. You have depth. In knowledge work, depth often matters more.

From Rigidity to Systematic Excellence

"Inflexible adherence to routines" reframes as "consistent implementation of proven procedures." "Difficulty with transitions" becomes "preference for sustained focus over constant context-switching." "Black-and-white thinking" transforms into "principled decision-making based on clear criteria."

These reframes aren't just positive thinking. They recognize that traits labeled as deficits in one context create advantages in others. The question isn't fixing your deficits but finding contexts where your processing style produces superior results.

Pattern Recognition and Systematic Thinking

Autistic brains often process patterns differently than neurotypical brains. You might notice details others miss. You identify systematic connections across apparently unrelated domains. You recognize when established patterns don't match current data.

Seeing What Others Miss

Many autistic people describe noticing details that others overlook. You see the inconsistency in the data. You recognize the logical flaw in the argument. You identify the pattern that predicts upcoming problems.

This pattern recognition proves particularly useful in analytical work, quality assurance, research, and strategic planning. Organizations need people who can see problems before they become crises and identify opportunities others miss.

The challenge: neurotypical colleagues might not immediately recognize the value of what you're seeing. They might dismiss your observations because they didn't notice the patterns themselves. Learning to present your pattern recognition effectively becomes a meta-skill—helping others see what you've already identified.

Systems-Level Analysis

Many autistic thinkers naturally analyze systems. You don't just see individual components—you see how they interact, where dependencies create vulnerability, and how changes in one area affect others.

This systems thinking applies across fields. In technology, you see how code modules interact. In healthcare, you understand how treatment protocols affect multiple body systems. In business, you recognize how operational changes ripple through supply chains and customer experience.

Organizations desperately need systems thinkers. Most people focus on their immediate domain without understanding broader

183

connections. Your natural systems analysis provides strategic advantage.

Case Study: Dr. Amara's Research Revolution

Dr. Amara worked as a neuroscience researcher. After her autism diagnosis at 41, she began recognizing how her autistic processing style contributed to her research success.

"I'd always been good at pattern recognition across large datasets. I would see connections that other researchers missed—relationships between variables that weren't obvious but proved significant when tested."

Her colleagues sometimes dismissed her observations initially. "They'd say 'that's an interesting hypothesis' in a tone suggesting they thought it was unlikely. But when I tested my hypotheses, they usually held up. I was seeing real patterns in data that looked random to others."

Dr. Amara realized her autism wasn't separate from her research excellence—it was fundamental to it. "My brain processes information differently. I notice details. I see patterns. I think systematically about how variables interact. These aren't compensation strategies—they're cognitive strengths that make me an excellent researcher."

She began framing her autism explicitly as an asset in grant proposals and research presentations. "I started describing my work as bringing neurodivergent analysis to neuroscience research. I positioned my different processing style as methodological advantage. And funders responded positively—they recognized the value of cognitive diversity in research teams."

Deep Focus and Flow States

The ability to focus intensely on tasks for extended periods appears frequently in autistic people. Neurotypical colleagues might struggle to maintain concentration for more than 20-30 minutes. You might enter flow states lasting hours.

The Concentration Advantage

Deep focus allows you to handle complex problems requiring sustained attention. Software development, scientific research, detailed analysis, creative work, and strategic planning all benefit from ability to maintain concentration without constant breaks.

This focus isn't just longer attention—it's qualitatively different engagement. You might lose track of time entirely. You might not notice hunger or fatigue. You're fully absorbed in the task.

The challenge: protecting this flow state from interruption. Open offices, meeting-heavy cultures, and constant communication expectations fragment the sustained concentration you need for your best work. Advocating for uninterrupted work time becomes essential.

Monotropic Processing

Some researchers describe autistic cognition as monotropic—tendency to focus attention intensely on a limited number of things at any given time. Neurotypical cognition is more polytropic—distributing attention across multiple simultaneous focuses.

Neither is superior. Monotropic processing creates disadvantages in environments requiring constant attention-shifting. But it creates advantages for tasks requiring sustained engagement with complex problems. Knowing your processing style helps you choose work that matches it.

Attention to Detail and Quality Standards

Many autistic people maintain high standards for accuracy, precision, and quality. You notice errors others miss. You care about getting things exactly right. You're uncomfortable with "good enough" when you know it could be better.

Quality-Driven Excellence

Your attention to detail and high standards produce work of exceptional quality. In fields where accuracy matters—scientific research, financial analysis, editing, engineering, medical diagnostics—your standards prevent errors and ensure excellence.

The challenge: neurotypical workplace cultures often prioritize speed over perfection. "Done is better than perfect" makes sense for some contexts but not all. Learning when to apply your high standards fully versus when to accept adequate work for low-stakes situations becomes necessary.

Continuous Improvement Mindset

Your awareness of how things could be better drives continuous improvement. You see inefficiencies in processes. You identify opportunities for optimization. You develop systems that work more effectively.

Organizations benefit enormously from employees who naturally identify improvement opportunities. The key is presenting improvements as enhancements to existing systems rather than criticism of current practices.

Case Study: Lucia's Quality Assurance Excellence

Lucia worked in software quality assurance. Her attention to detail and systematic testing approach made her exceptionally effective at finding bugs other testers missed.

"I would test edge cases that other people didn't think to check. I would notice inconsistencies in behavior that seemed minor but could cause major problems. I had detailed mental models of how the software should work and immediately noticed when actual behavior didn't match."

Her manager initially worried that Lucia was "too picky" about minor issues. "He'd say things like 'that's not a serious bug' or 'users probably won't notice that.' But I knew that small inconsistencies often indicated larger underlying problems."

Lucia started documenting how the seemingly minor issues she caught prevented major problems in production. "I created a log showing bugs I'd identified in testing that would have caused significant customer issues if they'd reached production. The data showed my 'pickiness' saved the company money."

Her thoroughness became recognized as an asset rather than excessive perfectionism. "Management started assigning me to critical projects where quality was especially important. They valued my attention to detail instead of seeing it as a problem."

Authentic Leadership and Principled Decision-Making

Autistic women often bring authenticity and clear ethical principles to leadership roles. You communicate directly. You make decisions based on consistent criteria rather than politics. You maintain high standards for yourself and others.

Values-Based Leadership

Many autistic people have strong sense of fairness and justice. You apply rules consistently. You don't play favorites. You make decisions based on principles rather than convenience or popularity.

This principled approach builds trust. People know where they stand with you. Your decisions are predictable and fair. You don't engage in the political maneuvering that makes many leadership environments toxic.

The challenge: principled leadership sometimes conflicts with organizational politics. You might refuse to bend rules that others see as flexible. You might call out unfairness even when speaking up creates difficulty for you. Maintaining your principles while working within imperfect systems requires strategic thinking.

Direct Communication in Leadership

Your direct communication style can be a leadership asset. You provide clear expectations. You give feedback straightforwardly. You don't leave people guessing about your thinking.

Many employees prefer direct managers to those who hint, imply, or speak ambiguously. Clear communication reduces anxiety and improves performance. Your communication style—presented as clarity rather than bluntness—can be framed as leadership strength.

Case Study: Dr. Helena's Academic Department Leadership

Dr. Helena became department chair at her university at age 52. She'd received her autism diagnosis five years earlier and decided to lead authentically rather than masking.

"I communicated directly with faculty. I set clear expectations. I applied policies consistently. I didn't engage in the usual academic politics where decisions happen in back channels and informal conversations."

Some colleagues found her style jarring initially. "They were used to chairs who implied things rather than stating them directly. My straightforward communication seemed harsh to people accustomed to more indirect approaches."

But many faculty appreciated the clarity. "Junior faculty particularly valued knowing exactly where they stood. I gave them clear feedback on tenure progress. I told them specifically what they needed to improve. They didn't have to guess or worry."

Dr. Helena's department developed reputation for transparency and fairness. "People trusted that I would apply policies consistently and make decisions based on merit rather than favoritism. That trust created a healthier department culture."

Finding Careers That Align With Your Special Interests

One of the most powerful career strategies for autistic women involves building professional life around your special interests. The intense focus and deep knowledge you've developed in your areas of interest can become the foundation for meaningful, sustainable work.

Special Interests as Career Foundations

Your special interests aren't hobbies to pursue in spare time—they're domains where you naturally excel. The knowledge you've accumulated, the focus you can sustain, and the genuine enthusiasm you bring to these areas create professional advantage.

Careers built on special interests provide intrinsic motivation. You're not forcing yourself to care about work—you're doing work you'd be thinking about anyway. This reduces the energy cost of work and increases sustainability.

Translating Interests Into Careers

Some special interests translate obviously into careers: fascination with computers becomes software development, interest in animals becomes veterinary medicine, passion for books becomes editing or library science.

Others require more creative translation: interest in train schedules might translate to logistics and supply chain management, fascination with specific historical periods could become academic research or museum work, intense focus on textile arts might become fashion design or textile conservation.

The question isn't if your interest has career applications but how to identify and pursue those applications.

Multiple Interest Integration

Some autistic women have sequential special interests—intense focus on one topic for months or years before shifting to another. This pattern might seem problematic for career stability. But it can create interdisciplinary expertise that combines knowledge from multiple domains in novel ways.

The biologist who was previously fascinated by programming might develop computational biology skills. The psychologist who studied art history might create specialized therapy using art analysis. Your varied interests create unique skill combinations.

Case Study: Vivienne's Entomology Enterprise

Vivienne had been fascinated by insects since childhood. She studied entomology in college but struggled to find work that matched her passion—most entomology jobs involved either academic research or pest control, neither of which suited her interests.

"I wanted to work with beneficial insects and help people appreciate insects' ecological importance. But there wasn't an obvious career path for that."

After her autism diagnosis at 33, Vivienne decided to create the career she wanted rather than trying to fit into existing options. She started a business providing insect identification services, native pollinator garden consulting, and educational programs about beneficial insects.

"I built a career entirely around my special interest. I spend my days identifying insects, designing pollinator habitats, teaching people about insect ecology. It's not just work that involves my interest—it is my interest, professionalized."

The business allows Vivienne to work with her natural processing style. "Most of my client interaction is asynchronous—email consultations, written reports. I do some in-person education programs but I control the frequency and format. I've designed work around both my interest and my autistic processing needs."

Building Businesses Around Your Neurodivergent Brain

Entrepreneurship offers autistic women opportunity to design work entirely around their strengths and needs. You control your environment, schedule, client interactions, and work processes. This control comes with challenges—income variability, responsibility for all business aspects, lack of external structure. But for many autistic women, the trade-offs are worthwhile.

Designing Work That Works

Self-employment allows you to optimize every aspect of work for your neurology. You choose: clients who communicate in ways that work for you, projects that align with your strengths, schedules that match your energy patterns, environments you control completely, and communication methods that suit your processing.

This level of control proves impossible in traditional employment. Employers have their requirements and your needs must fit within those constraints. Running your own business reverses this—work fits around your needs.

Managing Entrepreneurship Challenges

Self-employment introduces challenges autistic people might find particularly difficult: irregular income creating financial uncertainty, self-directed structure requiring executive function, marketing and sales requiring social skills, constant context-switching between business aspects, and isolation without automatic social contact.

Successful autistic entrepreneurs develop strategies for these challenges: building financial reserves to manage income variability, creating external structure through routines and systems, finding marketing approaches that suit their communication style, outsourcing or automating tasks outside their strengths, and deliberately building professional community.

Niche Specialization Strategy

Many successful autistic entrepreneurs find success through deep specialization. Instead of offering broad services to wide audiences, they become the expert in a specific niche. This plays to autistic strengths—deep knowledge, attention to detail, systematic approaches.

Specialization allows you to work with clients who specifically want your particular expertise. You're not competing on general skills but on specialized knowledge. Your deep interest in the niche becomes professional advantage rather than excessive focus.

Case Study: Sasha's Technical Writing Business

Sasha worked as a technical writer for software companies for 15 years. She excelled at translating complex technical concepts into clear documentation but struggled with open office environments and extensive collaboration requirements.

"After my autism diagnosis, I realized I could do the work I loved—technical writing—without the environmental challenges of traditional employment. I started freelancing."

Sasha specialized in API documentation for developer tools. "This ultra-specific niche let me become genuinely expert in one type of technical writing. Clients hired me specifically for API documentation expertise. I wasn't competing with every freelance writer—I was competing with the small number of API documentation specialists."

The business structure accommodated her needs perfectly. "I work from home. I communicate with clients asynchronously through email and project management tools. I control my schedule completely. I take projects that interest me and decline those that don't. I've designed work exactly around what I need."

Income took several years to stabilize. "The first few years were financially scary. But I built reserves and gradually developed steady client base. Now I earn more than I did in traditional employment while working fewer hours and experiencing far less exhaustion."

Case Study: Eloise's Research Consulting Practice

Eloise had a PhD in sociology and had worked as a university researcher. She loved research but found the academic environment—

teaching requirements, committee work, departmental politics—unsustainable.

"I wanted to do research without all the other aspects of academic life. I decided to offer independent research consulting."

Eloise works with nonprofit organizations, conducting research studies, analyzing data, and writing reports. "Organizations get high-quality research without hiring full-time research staff. I get to do the work I love without the academic environment's challenges."

The consulting work aligns perfectly with her strengths. "Research uses my systematic thinking, attention to detail, and ability to focus deeply on complex analysis. I work independently, which suits my processing style. Client interaction is limited and structured—initial meetings to define projects, interim check-ins, final presentations. I'm not managing ongoing relationships but completing defined projects."

Eloise maintains flexibility to prevent burnout. "I take fewer projects than I could if I was maximizing income. But I'm optimizing for sustainability. I have time to rest between projects. I decline work that would require excessive social interaction or tight deadlines that would push me into exhaustion. I'm thriving, not just surviving."

Success Stories of Autistic Women

Beyond the case studies throughout this book, countless autistic women have achieved remarkable professional success by working with their neurology rather than against it. These women redefined success on their terms rather than accepting conventional definitions.

Temple Grandin

Perhaps the most famous autistic woman professionally, Dr. Grandin revolutionized livestock handling through her unique visual thinking and deep understanding of animal behavior. She built a career as an animal science professor and consultant, becoming a prominent autism advocate. Her success demonstrates how autistic processing styles can create expertise that neurotypical approaches miss.

Scientists and Researchers

Many autistic women thrive in research fields where systematic thinking, attention to detail, and deep focus create advantage. They conduct groundbreaking research in physics, biology, mathematics, and other sciences. Their different processing styles lead to questions others don't ask and observations others don't make.

Artists and Creatives

Autistic women in creative fields bring unique perspectives and intense dedication to their work. They create art, music, literature, and other creative work that reflects their particular ways of experiencing the world. Their special interests often inform their creative practice, resulting in deep expertise in specific creative domains.

Business Leaders and Entrepreneurs

Autistic women have founded successful businesses, particularly in technology, consulting, and specialized services. They've built companies around their strengths, creating work environments that accommodate neurodivergent processing while producing excellent results.

The common thread: these women identified their strengths, found or created contexts where those strengths were assets, and built careers that worked with their neurology rather than demanding constant compensation.

Your Unique Contribution

You bring something to your workplace that neurotypical people can't. Your different processing style, your particular perspective, your specific combination of strengths—these create unique value.

The Cognitive Diversity Advantage

Teams composed entirely of neurotypical thinkers approach problems similarly. They have similar blind spots. They generate similar solutions. Adding neurodivergent thinkers increases cognitive diversity, which research shows improves problem-solving, innovation, and decision-making.

You're not just contributing despite your autism. You're contributing because of it. Your different thinking creates value precisely because it's different.

Innovation Through Different Processing

Innovation often comes from seeing connections others miss or questioning assumptions others accept. Your autistic processing style positions you to notice both. You see patterns in data others consider random. You question procedures others follow automatically. You identify problems others overlook.

Organizations that recognize this cognitive diversity advantage actively seek neurodivergent employees. They understand that different thinking styles produce better outcomes than homogeneous teams.

Building the Case for Your Value

Some organizations already recognize neurodiversity's value. Others need education. Building the case for your contributions requires documenting how your different processing creates results.

Track instances where your pattern recognition identified problems before they became critical. Document innovations that came from your different perspective. Show how your attention to detail prevented errors. Demonstrate that your systematic thinking improved processes.

This documentation serves multiple purposes: it proves your value to current employers, provides evidence for promotion discussions, builds your professional reputation, and helps educate organizations about neurodiversity's benefits.

From Surviving to Thriving

You've spent much of this book learning survival strategies—how to manage exhaustion, obtain accommodations, avoid burnout, and advocate for yourself. These strategies matter because you need to survive before you can thrive.

But survival isn't the end goal. Thriving means more than just avoiding breakdown. It means finding work that energizes rather than depletes you, building careers that align with your strengths, creating professional lives that feel sustainable long-term, and contributing meaningfully in ways that use your unique capabilities.

What Thriving Looks Like

Thriving varies individually, but common elements include: ending most workdays with energy remaining, feeling engaged by your work rather than just enduring it, using your strengths regularly in your role, having adequate recovery time built into your life, experiencing genuine professional relationships without constant masking, and feeling valued for your actual contributions rather than your performance of neurotypicality.

Thriving doesn't mean perfect conditions. It means sustainable conditions that allow you to function well long-term while remaining authentically yourself.

Writing Your Next Chapter

The professional path forward requires conscious choice about priorities and possibilities. You can't control all workplace factors, but you control more than you might think.

You choose which jobs to pursue and which to leave. You decide when to disclose autism and when to maintain privacy. You determine which accommodations to request and how to present them. You select which professional relationships to invest in and which to limit. You define what professional success means for you personally rather than accepting external definitions.

Writing your next chapter means making these choices intentionally based on self-knowledge, strategic thinking, and commitment to sustainability. You're not just reacting to circumstances but actively shaping your professional life.

The Future of Neurodivergent-Inclusive Workplaces

Workplace culture is changing—slowly and unevenly, but changing. Organizations increasingly recognize that diversity extends beyond visible characteristics to include cognitive diversity. They're beginning to understand that accommodating neurodivergent employees isn't just ethical obligation but business advantage.

Current Progress

Many large technology companies now have neurodiversity hiring programs. Professional organizations are developing resources about autism in the workplace. More autistic adults are openly autistic in professional settings. Research documents neurodivergent employees' strengths and appropriate supports.

This progress remains uneven. Small companies often lack resources for formal accommodation programs. Many managers still lack basic understanding of autism and accommodation. Discrimination persists despite legal protections.

But the direction of change favors inclusion. Each organization that implements successful neurodiversity programs demonstrates feasibility. Each openly autistic professional who succeeds challenges stereotypes. Each accommodation that improves performance makes the business case stronger.

Your Role in Change

Individual autistic women can't fix workplace ableism alone. But you contribute to change through your presence, advocacy, and success.

You make autism visible simply by existing openly in professional spaces. You educate colleagues through your willingness to explain your needs. You demonstrate autistic capability through your work.

You advocate for accommodations that help not just you but other neurodivergent employees.

Change happens through accumulated individual actions plus systemic advocacy. You're part of both. Your choice to request accommodations, disclose autism, or advocate for inclusive practices contributes to broader cultural shifts that benefit autistic women who come after you.

Building the Future

The future workplace you want to see won't appear automatically. It requires active creation through advocacy, education, and demonstration. Support neurodiversity initiatives in your organizations. Educate colleagues about autism in adults and particularly in women. Advocate for accommodations that benefit all neurodivergent employees. Mentor younger autistic professionals.

Document what works. Share successful accommodation strategies. Talk openly about autism in professional contexts when safe to do so. Build networks of neurodivergent professionals who support each other.

Your professional success matters not just for you but for the autistic women watching to see if they too can build sustainable careers while remaining authentically themselves.

Your Journey Forward

This book has provided frameworks for understanding your experiences as an autistic professional woman. You've learned about masking's costs, how to obtain diagnosis, ways autism manifests in women, workplace challenges you face, burnout patterns and prevention, unmasking processes, self-advocacy skills, work redesign strategies, and support systems to build. Finally, you've explored how to position your autism as professional strength rather than limitation to overcome.

The information here creates foundation, not destination. You'll continue learning about your specific needs, developing strategies that work for your circumstances, building professional life that suits your neurology, and refining your approach as you gain experience and self-knowledge.

You're not alone in this process. Thousands of autistic women are creating sustainable professional lives, supporting each other, and gradually changing workplace cultures. You're part of a growing movement of autistic women who refuse to accept that professional success requires destroying yourself through unsustainable masking.

Your autistic brain isn't broken. It processes information differently, and that difference creates both challenges and capabilities. Professional success comes not from fixing yourself but from finding or creating contexts where your processing style produces superior results. That's not settling or lowering standards—it's strategic career management that positions your strengths appropriately.

You have the knowledge now. The application requires time, practice, and patience with yourself as you experiment with different strategies and discover what works for you. Some approaches from this book will suit you perfectly. Others won't fit your specific circumstances. That's expected—take what's useful and leave what isn't.

The future of neurodivergent-inclusive workplaces depends partly on autistic women like you showing that different ways of thinking produce excellent results. Your success, your advocacy, and your willingness to be authentically autistic in professional spaces all contribute to change.

You've learned to survive. Now go thrive.

Where This Leaves You

The book ends, but your journey continues. You now possess frameworks for understanding your autistic experiences in professional contexts, strategies for managing common challenges, tools for advocating for yourself, knowledge about building support systems, and confidence that your neurological differences create value rather than just creating problems.

Apply this knowledge at your own pace. Experiment with strategies. Give yourself permission to succeed on your terms rather than others' definitions. Build professional life that sustains you long-term rather than burning bright briefly before collapse.

You deserve work that energizes rather than depletes you. You deserve to be known and valued for who you actually are. You deserve professional success without destroying your health. These aren't unreasonable demands—they're basic requirements for sustainable careers.

Go create that career. You have everything you need.

Key Takeaways

Strength Reframing

- Autistic traits labeled as deficits in one context create advantages in others

- Direct communication, intense interests, systematic thinking, and high standards all serve as professional strengths

- The question isn't fixing yourself but finding contexts where your processing style produces superior results

- Reframing requires changing your own perspective plus educating others about your strengths

Cognitive Advantages

- Pattern recognition allows you to see connections others miss and identify problems before they become critical

- Deep focus and flow states enable sustained concentration on complex problems

- Attention to detail and quality standards prevent errors and ensure excellence

- Systems-level thinking reveals connections and dependencies others overlook

Career Alignment

- Building careers around special interests provides intrinsic motivation and deep expertise

- Entrepreneurship allows complete control over environment, schedule, and work processes

- Niche specialization plays to autistic strengths in deep knowledge and systematic approaches

- Success comes from working with your neurology rather than constantly compensating

Leadership Capabilities

- Authentic leadership based on clear principles builds trust and consistency

- Direct communication provides clarity that many employees prefer to ambiguous management

- Values-based decision-making creates fair, predictable leadership

- Your communication style is an asset when framed as clarity rather than bluntness

Unique Contributions

- Cognitive diversity improves team problem-solving, innovation, and decision-making

- Your different processing style creates value precisely because it differs from neurotypical approaches

- Document your contributions to build case for your value and educate organizations

- Innovation often comes from questioning assumptions others accept automatically

Future Building

- Professional success matters not just for you but for autistic women watching to see if sustainable careers are possible

- Individual advocacy combined with systemic change gradually shifts workplace cultures

- Support neurodiversity initiatives, educate colleagues, and mentor younger autistic professionals

- You're part of growing movement creating possibilities that didn't exist before

Appendix A: Workplace Request Template

Template for Initial Accommodation Request

[Date]

[Supervisor/HR Representative Name] [Title] [Company Name] [Address]

Dear [Name],

I am writing to request workplace accommodations under the Americans with Disabilities Act. I have a medical condition that affects [brief functional description—e.g., "my sensory processing and concentration in certain environments"].

To perform my job effectively, I need the following accommodations:

1. [Specific accommodation—e.g., "Permission to wear noise-canceling headphones while working"]

   o This accommodation will help me by: [Explain functional benefit—e.g., "blocking distracting background noise so I can concentrate on complex analysis tasks"]

2. [Specific accommodation—e.g., "Flexible work-from-home options two days per week"]

   o This accommodation will help me by: [Explain functional benefit—e.g., "reducing sensory overload from the office environment and allowing me to work during my peak productivity times"]

3. [Specific accommodation—e.g., "Written meeting agendas provided at least 24 hours in advance"]

- This accommodation will help me by: [Explain functional benefit—e.g., "giving me time to process information and prepare substantive contributions"]

I have attached documentation from my healthcare provider confirming my need for these accommodations. I would like to schedule a meeting to discuss these requests and begin the interactive process.

I am committed to performing my job effectively and believe these accommodations will allow me to contribute at my highest level. Thank you for considering this request.

Sincerely,

[Your Name] [Your Title] [Contact Information]

Documentation to Include:

- Letter from healthcare provider confirming you have a condition qualifying as a disability under the ADA

- Specific language stating accommodations are medically necessary

- No requirement to disclose specific diagnosis

- Provider's contact information for verification if needed

Appendix B: Autistic Burnout Assessment Tool

Burnout Severity Assessment

Rate each statement on a scale of 0-4:

- 0 = Never/Not at all
- 1 = Rarely/Slightly
- 2 = Sometimes/Moderately
- 3 = Often/Considerably
- 4 = Always/Extremely

Exhaustion Indicators

1. I feel exhausted even after full night's sleep
2. I need significantly more recovery time after activities than I used to
3. I can't seem to catch up on rest no matter how much I sleep
4. Simple tasks feel overwhelming
5. I have no energy for activities I usually enjoy

Skill Loss Indicators

6. I forget tasks I used to remember easily
7. I make mistakes I wouldn't normally make
8. Skills I've had for years suddenly feel difficult
9. I struggle with executive function tasks (planning, organizing) more than usual

10. I have difficulty making decisions about simple things

Sensory Sensitivity Indicators

11. Sounds that didn't bother me before now feel intolerable

12. I'm more sensitive to lights, textures, or smells than usual

13. My sensory sensitivities have increased noticeably

14. I need to avoid sensory situations I previously managed

15. Environmental factors that were manageable now feel overwhelming

Social and Communication Indicators

16. I have less tolerance for social interaction than usual

17. Masking requires more effort than it used to

18. I experience more frequent shutdowns or meltdowns

19. I can't maintain my usual communication capacity

20. I need significantly more alone time to function

Scoring:

- 0-20: Low burnout risk. Implement prevention strategies.

- 21-40: Moderate burnout. Reduce demands and increase support.

- 41-60: Significant burnout. Immediate intervention needed— consider medical leave, therapy, and substantial demand reduction.

- 61-80: Severe burnout. Medical intervention essential. Cannot continue current level of demands.

If you score in the moderate to severe range, consult healthcare providers immediately. Burnout requires extended recovery time and reduced demands, not just rest.

Appendix C: Masking Inventory Checklist

Social Masking Behaviors

Check all behaviors you engage in regularly:

- Force eye contact during conversations

- Practice facial expressions to appear interested/friendly

- Suppress stims or engage in socially acceptable stims only

- Script conversations in advance

- Memorize phrases for common social situations

- Mirror other people's body language

- Pretend to understand jokes or references you don't get

- Laugh at appropriate times even if you don't find something funny

- Ask questions you already know answers to in order to seem engaged

- Modify your speech patterns to match others

Sensory Masking Behaviors

- Tolerate uncomfortable sensory input without showing distress

- Suppress reactions to painful sounds, lights, or textures

- Force yourself to eat foods you find sensorially unpleasant

- Endure physical discomfort from clothing or temperature
- Hide sensory overwhelm until you're alone
- Push through sensory overload instead of taking breaks
- Maintain composure in sensorially challenging environments

Communication Masking Behaviors

- Translate your direct communication into more indirect phrasing
- Add unnecessary pleasantries to straightforward requests
- Soften factual statements to avoid appearing blunt
- Pretend to need time to think about things you know immediately
- Phrase clear opinions as questions or suggestions
- Use vague language instead of specific descriptions

Cognitive and Emotional Masking

- Suppress your intense interests in conversations
- Pretend to care about topics you find boring
- Hide your confusion about social expectations
- Conceal difficulties with tasks others find easy
- Fake understanding of implied meanings
- Hide your genuine emotional responses

Workplace-Specific Masking

- Participate in social events you find exhausting
- Attend meetings you don't need to attend for appearance's sake
- Make small talk you find meaningless

- Pretend changes in routine don't bother you

- Hide your need for predictability and structure

- Avoid advocating for accommodations you need

Interpreting Your Results:

If you checked many items, you're likely masking extensively. This masking requires significant energy and contributes to exhaustion. Consider:

- Which masking behaviors serve protective functions versus which you could reduce?

- What would happen if you stopped some of these behaviors?

- How much energy would you reclaim by selective unmasking?

- Which contexts allow unmasking safely versus which require masking?

Use this inventory to guide unmasking decisions. Not all masking needs to stop immediately, but recognizing the full extent of your masking helps you make conscious choices about where to unmask first.

Appendix D: Energy Budget Worksheet

Daily Energy Capacity Assessment

Rate your typical daily energy capacity on a scale of 1-100, with 100 being your peak capacity and 1 being complete exhaustion.

My baseline daily energy capacity: _____

Energy Expenditure Tracking

List regular activities and rate the energy each requires:

Work Activities:

- Focused analytical work: _____ energy units per hour

- Meetings (in-person): _____ energy units per hour

- Meetings (virtual): _____ energy units per hour

- Email and written communication: _____ energy units per hour

- Phone calls: _____ energy units per hour

- Client/customer interaction: _____ energy units per hour

- Collaborative work: _____ energy units per hour

Personal Activities:

- Grocery shopping: _____ energy units

- Cooking: _____ energy units

- Household chores: _____ energy units

- Personal care routines: _____ energy units

- Social events: _____ energy units

- Family interaction: _____ energy units

- Commuting: _____ energy units per day

Recovery Activities:

List activities that restore energy:

- Solitude/alone time: +_____ energy units per hour

- Special interests: +_____ energy units per hour

- Sensory-friendly activities: +_____ energy units per hour

- Rest: +_____ energy units per hour

Budget Analysis:

Add up your daily energy expenditures for a typical workday:

Total daily expenditure: _____ Daily capacity: _____ Deficit/surplus: _____

If expenditures exceed capacity, you're operating unsustainably. Solutions include:

- Reduce energy-intensive activities

- Increase recovery time

- Request accommodations that reduce energy costs

- Redesign schedule to protect capacity

Weekly Energy Tracking:

Track actual energy levels throughout a week. Note:

- Starting energy level each morning

- Activities throughout the day

- Energy level at end of work

- Recovery activities

- Next morning's starting energy

Patterns will emerge showing which activities drain you most and how much recovery time you actually need.

Appendix E: Sensory Profile Guide

Auditory Sensitivities

Rate your sensitivity to each sound type (0 = no problem, 5 = extremely distressing):

- Background conversation: _____

- Fluorescent light buzzing: _____

- Traffic noise: _____

- Loud music: _____

- Phone ringing: _____

- Multiple people talking simultaneously: _____

- Sudden loud noises: _____

- Repetitive sounds (typing, tapping): _____

Accommodations for auditory sensitivities:

- Noise-canceling headphones

- White noise or ambient sound apps

- Workspace location away from noise sources

- Permission to decline calls in favor of written communication

Visual Sensitivities

Rate your sensitivity (0 = no problem, 5 = extremely distressing):

- Fluorescent lighting: _____

- Bright sunlight: _____
- Flashing or flickering lights: _____
- Computer screen brightness: _____
- Visual clutter: _____
- Movement in peripheral vision: _____
- Certain color combinations: _____

Accommodations for visual sensitivities:

- Desk lamp to replace overhead fluorescent lights
- Screen filters and brightness adjustment
- Sunglasses or tinted glasses
- Workspace with minimal visual distractions
- Permission to organize your space

Tactile Sensitivities

Rate your sensitivity (0 = no problem, 5 = extremely distressing):

- Certain fabric textures: _____
- Tags in clothing: _____
- Tight or restrictive clothing: _____
- Unexpected touch: _____
- Specific temperatures: _____
- Textures of certain materials: _____

Accommodations for tactile sensitivities:

- Flexible dress code allowing comfortable clothing
- Personal climate control devices

- Communication that your workspace is touch-free
- Permission to adjust furniture for comfort

Olfactory Sensitivities

Rate your sensitivity (0 = no problem, 5 = extremely distressing):

- Perfumes/colognes: _____
- Cleaning products: _____
- Food smells: _____
- Air fresheners: _____
- Strong scents generally: _____

Accommodations for olfactory sensitivities:

- Scent-free workplace policy
- Workspace location away from break room/kitchen
- Air purifier for your immediate area
- Communication with colleagues about scent sensitivities

Creating Your Sensory Profile Summary:

List your three highest-scoring sensitivities:

1. _____
2. _____
3. _____

For each, identify specific accommodations you need and how to request them.

Appendix F: Career Alignment Exercise

Identifying Your Strengths

List 5-10 things you do well:

1. _____
2. _____
3. _____
4. _____
5. _____

For each strength, note: Does this come naturally or require significant effort?

Natural strengths (things you do well with minimal effort) are your foundation for career alignment.

Special Interests Assessment

List current and past special interests:

1. _____
2. _____
3. _____
4. _____
5. _____

For each interest, consider:

- Have you maintained this interest long-term or was it intense but temporary?

- Do you have deep knowledge in this area?

- Could this interest translate into career applications?

Ideal Work Environment

Describe your ideal work environment across these dimensions:

Social interaction level:

- Mostly solitary work with minimal interaction

- Mix of independent and collaborative work

- Primarily collaborative work

Communication preferences:

- Written communication (email, documents)

- Verbal communication (meetings, calls)

- Mixed depending on context

Structure needs:

- Highly structured with clear procedures

- Moderate structure with some flexibility

- High autonomy with minimal structure

Sensory environment:

- Quiet with minimal sensory input

- Moderate sensory environment

- Can adapt to various environments

Schedule preferences:

- Highly consistent routine

- Some consistency with occasional variation
- Flexible schedule

Career Direction Analysis

Current role alignment assessment:

What percentage of your current work aligns with your strengths? _____% What percentage involves your special interests? _____% How well does your current environment match your ideal? (1-10): _____

If alignment is low (below 50% for strengths, below 30% for environment match), consider:

- Can current role be redesigned for better alignment?
- Would different position in same organization improve alignment?
- Does complete career change make sense?

Exploring Alternative Career Paths

Based on your strengths and interests, brainstorm 3-5 alternative career directions:

1. _____
   - How this aligns with strengths: _____
   - How this connects to interests: _____
   - Typical work environment: _____
   - Steps to transition: _____

2. _____

[Repeat analysis]

3. _____

[Repeat analysis]

Research these alternatives through: informational interviews with people in these roles, online research about typical duties and environments, shadowing or short-term projects to test fit.

Appendix G: Self-Advocacy Scripts

Script for Requesting Meeting Agenda in Advance

"I process information better when I have time to review it in advance. Could you send the meeting agenda and any relevant materials at least 24 hours before our meetings? This will allow me to prepare substantive contributions and make our meetings more productive."

Script for Requesting Written Communication

"I communicate most effectively in writing because it gives me time to process information and formulate clear responses. For important discussions, could we use email or shared documents rather than verbal conversations? I'm happy to have brief synchronous discussions for clarification, but I'd like the main communication to be written."

Script for Declining Optional Social Events

"Thanks for the invitation. I need to manage my energy carefully, and social events outside work hours aren't sustainable for me. I hope you have a great time."

If pressed: "I appreciate the invitation, but I've learned what my limits are and I need to respect them."

Script for Requesting Reduced Meeting Attendance

"I'd like to discuss my meeting attendance. I'm spending significant time in meetings, which leaves insufficient time for my primary work responsibilities. Could we identify which meetings are essential for me versus which I could skip? For meetings I don't attend, I'm happy to review notes and provide written input."

Script for Requesting Work-From-Home Options

"I'm requesting the ability to work from home [X] days per week. Working remotely allows me to control my environment for optimal concentration and reduces sensory fatigue from the office. My work performance and availability will remain consistent—I'll be online and responsive during work hours. This accommodation will allow me to work more effectively."

Script for Responding to Discrimination

"I have a disability protected under the ADA. I've requested reasonable accommodations that allow me to perform my job effectively. Denying these accommodations or treating me differently because of my disability is discrimination. I'd like to resolve this through the proper channels. Can we schedule a meeting with HR to discuss this?"

Script for Explaining Direct Communication Style

"I communicate directly and literally. What some might perceive as bluntness is actually clarity and efficiency. When I give feedback or state problems, I'm providing useful information, not criticizing people. This communication style helps me work effectively, and I find it prevents misunderstandings."

Script for Setting Boundaries With Demanding Colleague

"I have a limited capacity for [meetings/calls/collaborative work]. I need to protect time for [my primary responsibilities]. I can help you with this [specific way, at specific time], but I can't [what they're asking beyond your capacity]. Let's find a solution that works for both of us."

Appendix H: Resource Directory

National Organizations

Autistic Self Advocacy Network (ASAN) Website: autisticadvocacy.org Focus: Self-advocacy, policy advocacy, and resources by and for autistic people

Autism Women's Network Website: autismwomensnetwork.org Focus: Support and resources specifically for autistic women

Autism Society of America Website: autism-society.org Focus: Support, resources, and local chapters

National Autistic Society (UK) Website: autism.org.uk Focus: Support, information, and advocacy

Workplace Support Organizations

Job Accommodation Network (JAN) Website: askjan.org Focus: Free consulting on workplace accommodations

Neurodiversity @ Work Employer Roundtable Focus: Supporting employers in neurodiversity hiring

Books by Autistic Authors

- "Unmasking Autism" by Devon Price
- "The Unmasking Workbook for Autistic Adults" by Jessica Penot
- "Divergent Mind" by Jenara Nerenberg
- "Autism in Heels" by Jennifer Cook O'Toole

- "Nerdy, Shy, and Socially Inappropriate" by Cynthia Kim
- "Spectrum Women" edited by Barb Cook and Michelle Garnett
- "Women and Girls with Autism Spectrum Disorder" by Sarah Hendrickx
- "The Complete Guide to Asperger's Syndrome" by Tony Attwood

Online Communities

- r/AutismInWomen (Reddit)
- r/aspergirls (Reddit)
- Autistic Women and Girls Facebook groups
- Wrong Planet forums (www.wrongplanet.net)
- Yellow Ladybugs (Australia-based, yellow-ladybugs.com.au)

Diagnostic Resources

RAADS-R (Ritvo Autism Asperger Diagnostic Scale)

- Self-assessment tool with high accuracy for adults
- Available online through various autism resources

Autism Diagnostic Clinics

- Search for specialists in adult autism assessment
- Look for clinicians with experience in female presentations

Professional Associations

Association for Autistic Community (AAC)

- Professional development for autistic adults
- Networking and support

Neurodiversity in the Workplace Groups

- Check for local or industry-specific groups
- LinkedIn has numerous neurodiversity professional groups

Mental Health Resources

National Suicide Prevention Lifeline

- Phone: 988
- Available 24/7

Crisis Text Line

- Text HOME to 741741
- 24/7 text-based crisis support

Find Autism-Informed Therapists

- Psychology Today therapist finder (filter for autism specialization)
- AANE therapist directory
- Ask in autistic community groups for recommendations

Autism Research Centers

Yale Child Study Center

- Research on autism across lifespan

UCSF Autism Center

- Adult autism research and clinical services

Simons Foundation Autism Research Initiative (SFARI)

- Funding and conducting autism research

Legal Resources

Disability Rights Education & Defense Fund (DREDF) Website: dredf.org Focus: Legal advocacy for disability rights

Equal Employment Opportunity Commission (EEOC) Website: eeoc.gov Focus: Enforcing employment discrimination laws

Employment Law Resources:

- National Employment Lawyers Association (nela.org)

- Local disability rights organizations

- State bar association lawyer referral services

Using These Resources Effectively

Start with resources most relevant to your immediate needs. If you need workplace accommodations, begin with JAN and EEOC resources. If you need community support, try online groups before seeking in-person options. If you're seeking diagnosis, research specialists in your area who understand adult autism in women.

Don't try to use everything at once. Pick 2-3 resources that address your current priorities. As those needs are met, you can explore additional resources.

Share resources with others. When you find something helpful, pass it along to other autistic women. Building community involves sharing knowledge and support.

References

- American Psychiatric Association. (2013). *Diagnostic and statistical manual of mental disorders* (5th ed.). American Psychiatric Publishing.

- Americans with Disabilities Act of 1990, 42 U.S.C. § 12101 et seq. (1990).

- Attwood, T. (2007). *The complete guide to Asperger's syndrome*. Jessica Kingsley Publishers.

- Austin, R. D., & Pisano, G. P. (2017). Neurodiversity as a competitive advantage. *Harvard Business Review*, 95(3), 96–103.

- Bargiela, S., Steward, R., & Mandy, W. (2016). The experiences of late-diagnosed women with autism spectrum conditions: An investigation of the female autism phenotype. *Journal of Autism and Developmental Disorders*, 46(10), 3281–3294.

- Baron-Cohen, S. (2017). Editorial Perspective: Neurodiversity—a revolutionary concept for autism and psychiatry. *Journal of Child Psychology and Psychiatry*, 58(6), 744–747.

- Belcher, H. (2022). *Taking off the mask: Practical exercises to help understand and minimize the effects of autistic camouflaging*. Jessica Kingsley Publishers.

- Brown, C., Attwood, T., Garnett, M., & Stokes, M. A. (2020). Am I autistic? Utility of the Girls Questionnaire for Autism Spectrum Condition as an autism assessment in adult women. *Autism Research*, 13(9), 1554–1563.

- Cage, E., & Troxell-Whitman, Z. (2019). Understanding the reasons, contexts and costs of camouflaging for autistic adults. *Journal of Autism and Developmental Disorders*, 49(5), 1899–1911.

- Camm-Crosbie, L., Bradley, L., Shaw, R., Baron-Cohen, S., & Cassidy, S. (2019). "People like me don't get support": Autistic adults' experiences of support and treatment for mental health difficulties, self-injury and suicidality. *Autism*, 23(6), 1431–1441.

- Cassidy, S., Bradley, L., Shaw, R., & Baron-Cohen, S. (2018). Risk markers for suicidality in autistic adults. *Molecular Autism*, 9, Article 42.

- Cook, J., Hull, L., Crane, L., & Mandy, W. (2021). Camouflaging in autism: A systematic review. *Clinical Psychology Review*, 89, 102080.

- Dean, M., Harwood, R., & Kasari, C. (2017). The art of camouflage: Gender differences in the social behaviors of girls and boys with autism spectrum disorder. *Autism*, 21(6), 678–689.

- Dworzynski, K., Ronald, A., Bolton, P., & Happé, F. (2012). How different are girls and boys above and below the diagnostic threshold for autism spectrum disorders? *Journal of the American Academy of Child & Adolescent Psychiatry*, 51(8), 788–797.

- Equal Employment Opportunity Commission. (2011). *Regulations to implement the equal employment provisions of the Americans with Disabilities Act, as amended*. U.S. Equal Employment Opportunity Commission.

- Grandin, T., & Panek, R. (2013). *The autistic brain: Thinking across the spectrum*. Houghton Mifflin Harcourt.

- Hayward, S. M., McVilly, K. R., & Stokes, M. A. (2019). Challenges for females with high-functioning autism in the workplace: A systematic review. *Disability and Rehabilitation*, 41(19), 2289–2298.

- Hendrickx, S. (2015). *Women and girls with autism spectrum disorder: Understanding life experiences from early childhood to old age*. Jessica Kingsley Publishers.

- Hull, L., Levy, L., Lai, M.-C., Petrides, K. V., Baron-Cohen, S., Allison, C., Smith, P., & Mandy, W. (2021). Is social camouflaging associated with anxiety and depression in autistic adults? *Molecular Autism*, 12, Article 13.

- Hull, L., Petrides, K. V., Allison, C., Smith, P., Baron-Cohen, S., Lai, M.-C., & Mandy, W. (2017). "Putting on my best normal": Social camouflaging in adults with autism spectrum conditions. *Journal of Autism and Developmental Disorders*, 47(8), 2519–2534.

- Job Accommodation Network. (2023). *Workplace accommodations: Low cost, high impact*. Office of Disability Employment Policy, U.S. Department of Labor.

- Kim, C. (2014). *Nerdy, shy, and socially inappropriate: A user guide to an Asperger life*. Jessica Kingsley Publishers.

- Lai, M.-C., & Baron-Cohen, S. (2015). Identifying the lost generation of adults with autism spectrum conditions. *The Lancet Psychiatry*, 2(11), 1013–1027.

- Lai, M.-C., Lombardo, M. V., Ruigrok, A. N., Chakrabarti, B., Auyeung, B., Szatmari, P., Happé, F., & Baron-Cohen, S. (2017). Quantifying and exploring camouflaging in men and women with autism. *Autism*, 21(6), 690–702.

- Leedham, A., Thompson, A. R., Smith, R., & Freeth, M. (2020). "I was exhausted trying to figure it out": The experiences of females receiving an autism diagnosis in middle to late adulthood. *Autism*, 24(1), 135–146.

- Livingston, L. A., Shah, P., & Happé, F. (2019). Compensatory strategies below the behavioural surface in autism: A qualitative study. *The Lancet Psychiatry*, 6(9), 766–777.

- Lord, C., Rutter, M., DiLavore, P. C., Risi, S., Gotham, K., & Bishop, S. (2012). *Autism Diagnostic Observation Schedule, Second Edition (ADOS-2)*. Western Psychological Services.

- Mantzalas, J., Richdale, A. L., & Dissanayake, C. (2022). A conceptual model of risk and protective factors for autistic burnout. *Autism Research*, 15(6), 976–987.

- Miller, D., Rees, J., & Pearson, A. (2021). "Masking is life": Experiences of masking in autistic and nonautistic adults. *Autism in Adulthood*, 3(4), 330–338.

- Murray, D., Lesser, M., & Lawson, W. (2005). Attention, monotropism and the diagnostic criteria for autism. *Autism*, 9(2), 139–156.

- Nagib, W., & Wilton, R. (2020). Gender matters in career exploration and job-seeking among adults with autism spectrum disorder: Evidence from an online community. *Disability & Rehabilitation*, 42(18), 2530–2541.

- Nerenberg, J. (2020). *Divergent mind: Thriving in a world that wasn't designed for you*. HarperOne.

- North, A. S. (2021). Reconceptualising "reasonable adjustments" for the successful employment of autistic women. In M. Duckworth & R. Sissons (Eds.), *Autistic Community and the Neurodiversity Movement* (pp. 183–197). Palgrave Macmillan.

- O'Toole, J. C. (2018). *Autism in Heels: The untold story of a female life on the spectrum*. Skyhorse Publishing.

- Pearson, A., & Rose, K. (2021). A conceptual analysis of autistic masking: Understanding the narrative of stigma and the illusion of choice. *Autism in Adulthood*, 3(1), 52–60.

- Penot, J. (2024). *The unmasking workbook for autistic adults: Neuroscience-based practices to embrace your authentic autistic self.* New Harbinger Publications.

- Price, D. (2022). *Unmasking Autism: Discovering the new faces of neurodiversity.* Harmony Books.

- Raymaker, D. M., Teo, A. R., Steckler, N. A., Lentz, B., Scharer, M., Santos, A. D., Kapp, S. K., Hunter, M., Joyce, A., & Nicolaidis, C. (2020). "Having all of your internal resources exhausted beyond measure and being left with no clean-up crew": Defining autistic burnout. *Autism in Adulthood*, 2(2), 132–143.

- Ritvo, R. A., Ritvo, E. R., Guthrie, D., Ritvo, M. J., Hufnagel, D. H., McMahon, W., & Eloff, J. (2011). The Ritvo Autism Asperger Diagnostic Scale-Revised (RAADS-R): A scale to assist the diagnosis of autism spectrum disorder in adults. *Journal of Autism and Developmental Disorders*, 41(8), 1076–1089.

- Sedgewick, F., Hill, V., Yates, R., Pickering, L., & Pellicano, E. (2016). Gender differences in the social motivation and friendship experiences of autistic and non-autistic adolescents. *Journal of Autism and Developmental Disorders*, 46(4), 1297–1306.

- Seers, K., & Hogg, R. (2023). "Fake it 'till you make it": Authenticity and wellbeing in late diagnosed autistic women. *Feminism & Psychology*, 33(1), 52–71.

- Singer, J. (2016). *NeuroDiversity: The birth of an idea.* Amazon Kindle.

- Silberman, S. (2015). *NeuroTribes: The legacy of autism and the future of neurodiversity*. Avery.

- Wood-Downie, H., Wong, B., Kovshoff, H., Mandy, W., Hull, L., & Hadwin, J. A. (2021). Sex/gender differences in camouflaging in children and adolescents with autism. *Journal of Autism and Developmental Disorders*, 51(4), 1353–1364.

- Zener, D. (2019). Journey to diagnosis for women with autism. *Advances in Autism*, 5(1), 2–13.

www.ingramcontent.com/pod-product-compliance
Lightning Source LLC
Chambersburg PA
CBHW071420090426
42737CB00011B/1521